Finding Peace

IN DIFFICULT TIMES

Finding Peace

IN DIFFICULT TIMES

TED P. ASAY, PH.D
MARK D. OGLETREE, PH.D

CFI
An imprint of Cedar Fort, Inc.
Springville, Utah

ISBN 13: 978-1-4621-4304-7

Published by CFI, an imprint of Cedar Fort, Inc.
2373 W. 700 S., Springville, UT 84663
Distributed by Cedar Fort, Inc., www.cedarfort.com

Library of Congress Control Number: 2022935666

Cover design by Courtney Proby
Cover design © 2022 Cedar Fort, Inc.
Edited and typeset by Spencer Skeen

Printed in the United States of America

10 9 8 7 6 5 4 3 2 1

Printed on acid-free paper

To my wife and best friend, Laura. Thank you for your encouragement and all you have taught me about living peacefully.

Much love, Ted

To my loving wife, Janie, who has always been a great source of calm to me, and who has taught me how to relax while going one hundred miles per hour. Thank you, Janie, for helping me focus on the most important things in life, and let many of the "not-so-important-things" go by the wayside.

Love, Mark

CONTENTS

CONTENTS

INTRODUCTION

His peace will ease our suffering,
Bind up our broken hearts, blot out
Our hates, engender in our breasts a
Love of fellow men that will suffuse our
Souls with calm and happiness.

—President Heber J. Grant[1]

IF YOU ASKED A GROUP OF PEOPLE what they desire most in life, you would likely get a myriad of responses including success, health, happiness, money, security, and meaningful relationships, to name a few. While all of these are important and desirable, what most people actually seem to long for at a core level is a feeling of peace—a sense of being calm, confident, relaxed and safe, even when the world is filled with uncertainty and pressures of all kinds. When was the last time you felt a genuine sense of inner peace? If you have to pause and reflect on it, maybe it is not happening often enough.

When you think of peace, images of ocean waves, mountain waterfalls, laying in a hammock, listening to beautiful music, or just being still may come to mind. Unfortunately, consistent feelings of inner peace seem to be in short supply and are increasingly difficult to find and maintain in our modern day. In 1831 the Lord told the Prophet Joseph Smith that in the last days, the days in which we are living, "peace shall be taken from the earth."[2] There is abundant evidence all around us of the fulfillment of that statement.

For example, at the time of this writing the world is in the process of recovering from a global pandemic that has claimed millions of lives and disrupted economies and lifestyles worldwide. Many have suffered financial and job losses, others suffer from lingering feelings of loneliness and isolation, and some people continue to be fearful and uncertain about what the future will bring.

Add to this racial unrest, political tensions, conflict between nations and natural disasters, and it becomes clear that we live in a time when "the whole earth shall be in commotion, and men's hearts shall fail them."[3] We are also exposed to the deceptions and distractions of the adversary who seeks to disrupt our progress, impinge our confidence and hope, and deaden our sensitivity to the still, small voice that brings comfort and peace.

If all of this is not enough to create turmoil in us on a daily basis, we each live busy, fast paced and sometimes, frenetic lives. Stressful jobs, overscheduled families, financial concerns, relationship problems, noise and technology assaults, long commutes, inconsiderate people and myriad kinds of daily hassles constantly test our resilience and undermine our sense of well-being. We (Ted and Mark) both face these kinds of challenges each day, as you do, and sometimes our sense of peace seems to evaporate. Ted recalled:

A few months ago I found myself in a situation where I was feeling completely overwhelmed due to a confluence of work stress, a demanding church calling, family responsibilities, and unexpected involvements with two friends who needed immediate help with big problems. In addition, I was facing a time crunch for putting together a professional presentation which, ironically, focused on methods for reducing stress and finding peace. My anxiety and stress were skyrocketing, I was irritable and worried much of the time, and I began having doubts about my ability to cope with what was happening.

Mark shared this experience:

As I was completing High School in the early 1980s, American Hostages were imprisoned in Iran, there were cold war threats bearing down upon our Country, gas prices had recently reached over a dollar a gallon, interest rates were in double-digits, and newly elected President Ronald Regan had just been shot. Many of my peers (including myself) wondered if we would ever graduate from college, marry, and raise our own children. It seemed that in 1980, the end of the world was right around the corner.

We have probably all had similar episodes in our lives that seemed overwhelming and strained our coping capacities. For some, this is not just a once in a while occurrence, but a frequent scenario that includes high levels of anxiety and stress that saps their emotional, physical and spiritual strength and dampens their ability to enjoy life.

As evidence of this, recent statistics indicate that 19 percent of American adults between the ages of 18-64 will have a diagnosable anxiety disorder this year—that's over 40 million or one-fifth of the adult population—and 31 percent will be affected by anxiety during their lifetime.[4] Just as concerning are studies on anxiety in youth that indicate prevalence rates of 12 percent.[5]

While some of the stress and anxiety we experience is the result of outside influences, some of it flows from the workings of our minds and how we react to what is happening around us. Our minds are marvelous and efficient at processing data at lightning fast speeds and encoding in our memories important information for future use. However, they also contribute to our anxiety and discontent by naturally gravitating toward a focus on the future or the past and distorting our perceptions of both. To be sure, remembering the past and anticipating the future are important in helping us to learn and progress, but we often spend unnecessary amounts of time fretting about the future and rehashing our past failures and regrets.

For example, you may notice yourself on any given morning having thoughts such as, "What if I am not able to get my project done?"

"What if my boss is in a bad mood?" or "Alex better not have a date with that same boy tomorrow night." More broadly, you might find yourself worrying about such things as, "Will I be successful?" "What if I don't have enough money?" or "Can I endure to the end?"

Commenting on our penchant for worrying about the future and becoming preoccupied with "what if's", Christian author Max Lucado observed:

> *Anxiety is a meteor shower of what-ifs. What if I don't close the sale? What if we don't get the bonus? What if we can't afford braces for the kids? What if my kids have crooked teeth? What if crooked teeth keep them from having friends, a career, or spouse? What if they end up homeless and hungry, holding a cardboard sign that reads, "My parents couldn't afford braces for me?" . . . Anxiety and fear are cousins but not twins. Fear sees a threat. Anxiety imagines one. Fear screams, "Get out!" Anxiety ponders, "What if?"*[6]

Conversely, your mind might shift to a focus on the past and drift into such thoughts as, "I can't believe I said that last night," "I should never have taken that job," or "I have made some real mistakes as a parent." Concerns about the past might also take the form of ruminating about past failures and losses, such as returning home early from a mission, going through a divorce, failing at a job or business, or experiencing past mistreatment or abuse.

Too much time in the past or the future ratchets up our fears, pulls down our moods and interferes with our enjoyment of the present. Our feelings of well-being and confidence are also compromised by comparing ourselves to others, excessive self-criticism, expecting too much from ourselves and others, feeling disconnected to people, and experiencing distance in our relationship with God.

With all that is going on in the world and in our personal lives to create worry and unrest, how do we reclaim our serenity and calmness? Where can we find inner peace?

There are a blessed few people, and we probably all know them, who seem to naturally be peaceful and content. After studying these individuals, Psychologist Jack Kornfield humorously pointed out:

If you can sit quietly after difficult news, if in financial down-turns you remain perfectly calm, if you can see your neighbors travel to fantastic places without a twinge of jealousy, if you can happily eat whatever's put on your plate and fall asleep after a day of running around without a drink or a pill, if you can always find contentment just where you are, you are probably a dog.[7]

For most of us who are human, the path to peace does not come quite as easily. We have little control over the tragedies and disasters that happen in the world, and sometimes little control over the events and challenges we face in life. However, we do have control over the way we perceive and respond to what happens around us and to us. We also determine how we respond to ourselves and interact with others, and we have great influence over the kind of relationship we have with God and the role he plays in our lives.

In this book we present several strategies that have been shown, either through scientific research or revealed truths, to increase our capacity to experience peace and well-being. These include learning to live more fully in the present, looking to the future with optimism and hope, and overcoming the effects of our past injuries, disappointments, and regrets. We also offer suggestions for cultivating the quality of self-compassion, taming perfectionism, using humor, managing stress and anxiety, and developing relationships that are healthy and healing. Finally, we focus on the importance of establishing a peaceful lifestyle, acquiring Christlike attributes, and relying on Jesus Christ, the "Prince of Peace."

These "small and simple" practices are the key to experiencing greater peace and enjoyment. We also understand that it is not practical, or helpful, to try to integrate all of these strategies into your life at the same time. We suggest that you decide which strategy you would like to try first and then gradually implement it in a way that works for you. Others can be added when you are ready. Additionally, we recognize that the practices we are suggesting are not a replacement for professional treatment. If the difficulties you are experiencing interfere with your daily functioning or cause you significant distress, we recommend that you consult with a mental health professional.

It is our hope that the ideas and suggestions contained in this book will help you to more effectively deal with the daily anxieties, worries and stresses you face and enable you to gain a greater measure of peace in your life. We also affirm that our greatest source of healing power is Jesus Christ, and we have confidence in his promise to those who follow him: "Peace I leave with you, my peace I give unto you: not as the world giveth, give I unto you. Let not your heart be troubled, neither let it be afraid."[8]

References to the Introduction

1   President Heber J. Grant, *Teachings of Presidents of the Church: Heber J. Grant* (2002), 226.

2   D&C 1:35.

3   D&C 45:26.

4   National Institute of Mental Health, https://www.nimh.nih.gov/health/statistics/any-anxiety-disorder.shtml.

5   JAMA Pediatrics, https://jamanetwork.com/journals/jamapediatrics/fullarticle/2782796.

6   Max Lucado, *Anxious for Nothing: Finding Calm in a Chaotic World* (Thomas Nelson: Nashville, TN, 2017).

7   Cited by Ronald Siegal in "The Science of Mindfulness: A Research Based Path to Well-Being," video series in The Great Courses, 2014.

8   John 14:27.

Chapter 1

LIVING IN THE PRESENT

The past is behind—learn from it;
The future is ahead—prepare for it;
The present is here—live in it.

—President Thomas S. Monson [1]

ONE OF THE most valuable skills you can develop in your quest for finding peace is the ability to live in the present. This might sound like a simple task, but it is anything but easy. As we move through each day, our minds naturally drift from a focus on what is happening in the present moment to concerns about the future—what is going to happen, or the past—what has happened, or how we are performing in comparison to others, or what tasks we need to complete. Much of our mental energy is spent on worrying, planning, anticipating, and rehashing our life experience.

"I wish I would have made better decisions growing up," "What if one of our children decides to leave the church?," and "It would sure be nice if I was back on that Caribbean cruise right now" are examples of the kinds of thoughts that dance on the stage of our minds. Our goal with this thinking is to try to anticipate or avoid uncomfortable experiences and emotions, rectify past experiences that bother us or transport ourselves into someplace that seems more pleasant than the present. While this is a normal and potentially helpful process, all too often our preoccupation with these concerns causes our minds to stray from awareness and enjoyment of what is happening now, in the present moment.

Living in the Present and Happiness

Ironically, when our minds wander, presumably in an effort to solve a concern or take us to a more pleasant place, we do not experience any increase in happiness or feelings of peace. In fact, there is scientific evidence that indicates just the opposite. In a study conducted by Matthew Killingsworth and Daniel Gilbert at Harvard University, the results revealed that a wandering mind is associated with decreased feelings of happiness.[2]

In their study, Killingsworth and Gilbert asked participants at random intervals how happy they were, what they were doing, and if they were thinking about what they were doing. Results of the study revealed that on average adults reported that their minds were wondering 47 percent of the time indicating that, to a surprising degree, their mental lives were focused on the non-present. Furthermore, people reported being the happiest when they were thinking about what they were doing presently and experienced the lowest levels of happiness when their minds were wandering.

The important message of this creative study is that when we are fully engaged in the present moment and thinking about what we are doing—no matter what it is—we are the happiest. This means that if you are simply chopping celery in the kitchen, but 100 percent engaged in the task, then you are much more likely to be feeling happy than if you are daydreaming about what you would rather be doing. You have probably had your own personal experience of avoiding doing something because it seemed hard or uninteresting, but once you got into it and gave it your full effort and attention, it actually became enjoyable.

There are likely several reasons why this is the case. First, when you are fully engaged in the here and now you are able to relieve your mind of unproductive "chatter" and the burden of worrying about the past, the future and concerns about how you are performing. You are also able to enjoy the intrinsic value of the moment to moment experience of whatever it is you are engaged in doing. In addition, when you tune into the present moment you are more focused and your mind is clearer which increases your productivity resulting in greater happiness. Finally, when you are engaged in interactions with others, being more present allows you to become more immersed in the reciprocal sharing of ideas and feelings which leads to a more fulfilling interpersonal experience.

Roadblocks to the Present

At this point you might be asking yourself, "If living in the present brings peace and happiness, then why don't we do it more?" The answer seems to be a combination of the natural tendency of our minds to wander, along with the myriad forces that pull us away from the present moment. One of these is our preoccupation with staying busy and relentlessly pursuing the completion of tasks and goals. Accomplishment, achievement, and goal attainment are, of course, important to succeeding in life. However, when your attention is always on accomplishing the next thing, achieving the next goal, staying busy, multitasking, and believing that your happiness will ultimately come down the road when you have finally done enough, then you are in danger of becoming overstressed, burned out and unhappy. Moreover, you deprive yourself of experiencing what is happening right now—in the present moment—that could be a rejuvenating source of happiness, peace, and enjoyment.

Another major influence that pulls us away from the present is our pervasive use of electronic devices. Computers, smart phones, tablets, televisions, and video games constantly bombard us with stimuli and noise of all kinds that hijack our attention and crowd out our awareness of what is happening all around us. You don't have to look too far to find some people who are so riveted on their electronic devices that they have no idea what else is going on around them. This is especially bothersome if they are also driving a car or are supposed to be involved in a face-to-face conversation.

As with many things, electronics can be both helpful and detrimental. Smart phones and tablets are wonderful at helping us communicate and stay connected to others. At the same time, they can create a need for constant stimulation, erode our ability to concentrate, and dull our appreciation for what is happening around us right now, in this moment.

Tips for Staying in the Present

The message we are trying to convey is that the ability to stay in the present moment is associated with increased peace, contentment, and happiness. To truly be convinced of this you have to experience it firsthand—you have to spend time in the present, that is, intentionally bring your attention to the present moment. How do you do this?

Monitor Your Attention

The best place to start is to become more aware of where your mind is at any given moment. Where is your attention right how? Are you focusing on the here and now or are you distracted and thinking about something else? Try bringing your mind back to the present when you notice that it has moved to some other place and reorient your attention to what is going on in front of you right now. For example, if you are talking to your spouse or a friend you might notice that you are thinking about something else, like where you will be eating dinner tonight. At that point, gently pull your mind back to the present and focus on the conversation. It is important in this process to have patience with yourself. Our minds are like puppy dogs and have to be repeatedly pulled back and gradually trained to stay in the present. This is a skill that, like learning to play a musical instrument, takes time and consistent effort to develop.

Focus on Your Surroundings

Another exercise that helps you stay in the present is focusing your mind on your surroundings. For example, try taking a walk and intentionally pay attention to what is around you. Notice the structures, the buildings, or houses; look up at the sky, the trees, and the flowers. Listen to the sounds around you—voices, music, automobiles, the chirping of birds. Tune into your tactile experience—the breeze as it touches your face and the temperature.

You will probably find that as you are trying to keep your mind in the present, there will be a tendency to slip back into thinking about other things, such as what you are going to do when you finish the walk, the unfinished tasks you have waiting for you, or what is going to happen tomorrow. When this happens just realize that it is part of the process of learning to be present and gently pull your mind back into the present moment.

For example, Ted recalls the following experience:

I was driving back from a church youth activity that had taken place at a beautiful lake that was located about two hours away from the city where I live. It was early in the morning and the sun was just coming up over the hills illuminating the landscape filled with trees, bushes, and other foliage. It was a beautiful sight, but as I drove along my mind became emerged in thinking about the church meeting that I was going to be speaking in the next day. I began thinking about all of the possible subjects that I might talk about and how I would present them. After several minutes of doing that, it dawned on me that I had lost contact with the present moment. I was so caught up in my concerns about the events of the next day, that I was not enjoying what I could be experiencing right now in this moment. I quickly turned my attention back to the scene in front of me—the beautiful trees, the cool air blowing through the window, and the serenity of the moment—which I very much enjoyed. Once I hit the interstate highway there was plenty of time to think about my talk.

Be Present in Daily Activities

You can also practice being present while doing routine tasks. For example, try to stay in the here and now when you brush your teeth, walk the dog, or prepare a meal. As you engage in the activity, try to notice the details of what you are doing and what it is like for you to do it. For example, when brushing your teeth, try to notice the taste of the toothpaste, what it feels like to brush each tooth, and the sensation of the water in your mouth.

Recreational activities also provide a nice opportunity to work on being present. These might include exercising, gardening, or playing a game. As an example, Elder Dieter F. Uchtdorf recounted the following experience of riding bicycles with his wife:

> My wife, Harriet, and I love riding our bicycles. It is wonderful to get out and enjoy the beauties of nature. We have certain routes we like to bike, but we don't pay too much attention to how far we go or how fast we travel in comparison with other riders.
>
> However, occasionally I think we should be a bit more competitive. I even think we could get a better time or ride at a higher speed if only we pushed ourselves a little more. And then sometimes I even make the big mistake of mentioning this idea to my wonderful wife.
>
> Her typical reaction to my suggestions of this nature is always very kind, very clear, and very direct. She smiles and says, "Dieter, it's not a race; it's a journey. Enjoy the moment." How right she is! Sometimes in life we become so focused on the finish line that we fail to find joy in the journey.[3]

In your efforts to stay present in your daily activities, try to do it without texting, talking on the phone or getting caught up in planning future events or trying to solve a problem that has come up. As you improve in staying in the moment, you will likely find that your productivity and problem solving abilities will improve also.

Finally, practice being present when you are interacting with others. While most of us enjoy communicating with our friends and family members, it is uncommon for us to be fully present when carrying on a conversation with another person. Instead of paying close attention to what the other person is trying to communicate, we are often focused on what we are going say back to them, or we may be bored or disinterested and are thinking about something completely different.

You can practice being present by trying to focus your attention solely on the other person and what they are saying. Try to tune in to the message they are communicating without judgment but with an interest in understanding. People can usually sense how tuned in another person is in the interaction and it is a gratifying experience to talk to someone who is fully present with you.

Take a Break from Screens

To be present at any moment you have to be aware of what is happening around you and how you are experiencing it. For all of its helpful aspects, technology can be a major roadblock to doing this. Our smartphones, iPads and computer games are attention grabbers and effectively pull our minds from a focus on the present. To get a sense of how much technology intrudes itself onto the stage of our minds, and to experience the liberating effect of being away from it for a brief time, try taking a break from electronics, and go on a technology fast for one day or for a few hours. During this time disengage from screens and devices and focus on the people you interact with, the tasks at hand, however mundane, and try to connect with the world around you.

A case in point occurred with one of Ted's sons:

A few years ago, my twenty-two-year old son took a four-week trip to Italy with a friend. Before leaving he decided he was going to discard all social media and only use his cell phone for calls or texting that were essential for continuing the trip, such as calling for hotel reservations and for emergencies. After returning home he recounted how exhilarating and enjoyable the trip was without the distraction of social media. He felt more engaged with the people he met, experienced the beautiful scenery at a deeper level and wasted much less time.

In a worldwide youth devotional in June 2018, President Russell M. Nelson invited the youth of the church "to enlist in the youth battalion of the Lord" and then asked them to do five things, the first one being to "disengage from a constant reliance on social media by holding a seven-day fast from social media." He then went on to explain why he was making this request:

If you are paying more attention to feeds from social media than you are to the whisperings of the Spirit, then you are putting yourself at spiritual risk—as well as the risk of experiencing intense loneliness and depression. . . . Another downside of social media is that it creates a false reality. Everyone posts their most fun, adventurous, and exciting pictures, which create the erroneous impression that everyone except you is leading a fun, adventurous, and exciting life. Much of what appears in your various social media feeds is distorted, if not fake. So give yourself a seven-day break from fake! Choose seven consecutive days and go for it! See if you notice any difference in how you feel and what you think, and even how you think, during those seven days. After seven days, notice if there are some things you want to stop doing and some things you now want to start doing.[4]

President Nelson's challenge for youth to take a break from social media was later extended to the women of the church[5] and would certainly be advisable for the men. A social media fast could lead to helpful insights about the impact of technology on both your spirituality and your ability to experience and enjoy the present moment.

In addition to taking a break from social media, there is a need to manage the impact of technology on a daily basis. One thing you could consider doing would be to limit the number of times you check messages and social media during the day. Some people are constantly checking their phones for posts, tweets, pics, and texts. One college student admitted that he has great difficulty focusing on his studies because he is constantly anticipating the next phone chime alerting him to an incoming message. One solution to the ongoing distraction of chimes and messages is to restrict checking to three times a day and doing it only at pre-determined times. Turning off notifications and taking social media off your main page area are also useful suggestions.

Be Still

An important prerequisite to living in the present is feeling calm and quiet in your mind. There are many ways to do this beginning with daily activities, such as listening to music, reading a book and taking a slow walk. There are also more formal ways including deep breathing and meditation. Deep breathing is an easy way to relax that can be done most anywhere and at any time. It consists of inhaling slowly through your nose, concentrating on your breath and noticing what is in your mind. This is followed by slowly exhaling through your mouth and letting your thoughts go out with your breath. Some people find it helpful to count as they are inhaling and exhaling.

In mindfulness meditation you center your awareness and attention internally to calm and clear your mind. You begin by focusing on your breathing and then noticing but not getting entangled in the thoughts that are in your mind and the sensations you are experiencing in your body. There are other helpful practices, including yoga and progressive muscle relaxation, that could be used to create stillness and relaxation. The important thing is to find something that works for you and then practice it consistently to get the best results.

There are also spiritual methods that can help to calm your mind and sharpen your awareness of the present. In Psalm 46:10 the Lord says, "Be still and know that I am God." The word "still" suggests a state of calm and quiet, where the noise of the world and our preoccupations with tasks are set aside. This is best achieved by finding a consistent time and place to "be still," to tune out the bustle and distractions of the world and to turn inward.

In an address to the young adults of the church, Elder M. Russell Ballard said,

> As an Apostle, I now ask you a question: Do you have any personal quiet time? . . .
>
> It is important to be still and listen and follow the Spirit. We simply have too many distractions to capture our attention, unlike any time in the history of the world. Everyone needs time to meditate and contemplate. . . . We all need time to ask ourselves questions or to have a regular personal interview with ourselves. We are often so busy and the world is so loud that it is difficult to hear the heavenly words "be still, and know that I am God."[6]

During the Savior's ministry on earth, he would occasionally take time out of his daily focus on teaching, healing, comforting, and loving and retreat to a place of solitude and quiet where he could leave the demands of the world and spend time resting and communing with his Heavenly Father.[7]

Being "still" also includes various spiritual practices such as prayer, reading, and pondering scripture; spiritual reflection; and having an openness to the what the Lord might want to say to you in the here and now through the "still, small voice" of the Holy Ghost. Being "present" in your relationship with God involves shifting to a spiritual state of mind and intently listening to what he might desire to communicate to "you in your mind and in your heart."[8] In describing this process, President Russell M. Nelson has counseled:

> Pray in the name of Jesus Christ about your concerns, your fears, your weaknesses—yes, the very longings of your heart. And then listen! Write the thoughts that come to your mind. Record your feelings and follow through with actions that you are prompted to take. As you repeat this process day after day, month after month, year after year, you will "grow into the principle of revelation."[9]

As we learn to become more present with God, more open to his communications, and more willing to align our desires with his, the Holy Ghost will change our hearts and we will be become more peaceful people, more like the Savior.

Learning to live in the present requires consistent daily effort and focus. As you intentionally strive to cultivate this skill you will find yourself gradually becoming more calm, less stressed, and able to enjoy a greater sense of peace.

References to Chapter 1

1   Thomas S. Monson, "Go For It," *Ensign*, May 1989.

2   Matthew Killingsworth and Daniel Gilbert, "A Wandering Mind Is an Unhappy Mind," *Science*, November 12, 2010, 932.

3   Dieter F. Uchtdorf, "Of Regrets and Resolutions," *Ensign*, November 2012.

4   Russell M. Nelson and Wendy W. Nelson, "Hope of Israel," *Worldwide Youth Devotional*, June 3, 2018.

5   Russell M. Nelson, "Sister's Participation in the Gathering of Israel," *Ensign,* November 2018.

6   M. Russell Ballard, Be Still and Know That I Am God," CES Devotional for Young Adults (San Diego), May 4, 2014.

7   See Matthew 14:23

8   D&C 8:2

9   Russell M. Nelson, "Revelation for the Church, Revelation for Our Lives," *Ensign*, May 2018.

Chapter 2

MAKING PEACE WITH THE PAST

Those who cannot remember the past are condemned to repeat it.

—George Santayana[1]

OUR ABILITY TO live in the present and to enjoy peace and well-being in life is closely tied to how we view the events of our personal past. We all have experienced a past filled with circumstances that were happy, affirming, and growth promoting as well as others that were sad, painful, disappointing, unfair, and sometimes even traumatic. Psychological science has taught us that our perspective regarding our past experiences has an important influence on how we currently view ourselves and others, how we interact with those around us, our motivation to achieve, our level of happiness and our emotional resilience.

For example, you can probably think of an experience you had during your formative years that has had significant impact on your current feelings about yourself. Perhaps you can recall a time when someone showed you unusual or unexpected kindness, or maybe a time when you felt embarrassed or humiliated. We are often most affected by a series of experiences with a particular person.

When children feel loved and securely attached to parents and other adults, it bodes well for their long-term development and happiness. At the same time, there are life-long negative ramifications for children who are raised in abusive or neglectful environments. Since our past experiences clearly affect the present, it is helpful to understand the connection between what has happened previously in our lives and who we are today. When these connections are made, it can give us feelings of continuity and coherence, which strengthens our sense of identity. In addition, as we look back and review our personal life timelines, we can see more clearly how we have changed, which may give us confidence to move forward with the expectation that we can continue to progress in our development.

Becoming Stuck in the Past

On the other hand, people sometimes get stuck in the past and are bogged down with unresolved feelings about previous experiences. Often, negative feelings are directed towards parents, siblings, other relatives, and friends. Preoccupations and angst about hurts, regrets, losses, and mistreatment consumes much of their mental energy and interferes with their personal effectiveness and enjoyment of the present. People who have felt betrayed or wronged may become obsessed with enacting justice or getting revenge on those who hurt them. Others struggle with feelings of guilt and shame about mistakes, weaknesses, sins, and times when they fell short and did not meet their own expectations. In one instance, a mother of three suffered from persistent guilt and self-denigration over having a depressive episode a few years earlier that she believed was damaging to her children.

Unresolved losses of many types can also lead to being stuck in the past. The death of a family member, divorce, loss of a close friendship, moving, lost opportunities, and watching children grow up and leave home, sometimes choosing paths that lead away from God, and many other experiences of loss permeate our lives. If these losses are not resolved, they can lead to longstanding feelings of grief, guilt, shame, and depression, and leave suffering people floating in a sea of "what ifs" and "if onlys."

Overcoming the Past

Most of the negative, painful, or regretful episodes from your past are usually worked out or in some way resolved or simply forgotten. However, for many there are bothersome memories and emotions that continue to periodically intrude themselves onto the stage of their consciousness, causing discomfort and turmoil. Unresolved issues from the past can cause you to think and act in ways that you dislike, do not understand well, and wish you could change. Overcoming the past first requires a willingness to remember and reflect on past experiences and how they affect you in the present. Remember that those who do not remember the past often repeat it.

It is also important to understand that the issue is not necessarily about what events occurred in the past—that is not the root of the problem. Instead, our relationship to what happened—our interpretation of the event—is most often the cause of our troubles. Similarly, what we learn from the past and what we do about it is more important that what happened.

Revisiting What Happened

Once you have made a conscious decision to address and work to overcome some aspect of your past, the next step is to identify the past experiences that affected you in an adverse way and that are still unresolved. This can be a challenging process because these experiences may involve loss, rejection, failure, sin, abuse, or trauma, along with associated feelings of sadness, grief, guilt, regret, shame, humiliation, fear and anger. Furthermore, your memory of these events may be dim or fuzzy. Seeking help from the Lord through the Holy Ghost can assist you in remembering important aspects of what happened and how you felt about it. Jesus taught this truth to His followers:

> But the Comforter, which is the Holy Ghost, whom the Father will send in my name, he shall teach you all things, and bring all things to your remembrance.[2]

In addition to helping you remember the past, the Holy Ghost can also provide comfort and strength as you proceed.[3]

As you recall past experiences and feelings, it is helpful to engage in some type of emotional processing of the event, where you have a chance to express what happened and how it made you feel. One often-used technique is expressive writing. In this approach, you simply write down all the thoughts, feelings, and reactions you have about a particular event or situation in a stream of consciousness style—without censoring it. This exercise can be completed in a private notebook or journal—for your eyes only. Others might get more benefit from verbally expressing their feelings to a trusted person, such as a close friend, spouse, church leader, or therapist.

A simple example of this process occurred in Ted's life as he was driving home from work on a Halloween evening:

As I was driving through our neighborhood, I saw young children dressed up in their Halloween costumes excitedly walking through the streets escorted from door to door by their parents who were clearly enjoying the experience. Suddenly, I felt sadness welling up in me and, to my surprise, tears came to my eyes. I was taken back by the experience and after a few moments of reflection, I realized that my tears had to do with missing our three children, the youngest of whom had left for college just two months earlier, leaving my wife and me as "empty nesters." Pleasant memories of walking through those same streets with our children on Halloween came back to me, along with pangs of loss and sadness. This experience helped me to become more aware of the emotional impact on me when our children left home, something I was mostly unaware of and probably avoiding. It also gave me an opportunity to feel the emotions I had about it and deal with the associated grief. Once I got home, I shared the entire event with my wife. She assisted me in processing my feelings of sadness on a deeper level and helped me move down a path toward eventual resolution of my experience of loss.

It should be noted that if you have had past experiences that involved significant trauma (abuse, assault, rape, military combat, serious accident, etc.), or if you are currently experiencing high levels of anxiety or depression, we suggest you first consult with a qualified mental health professional (psychologist, professional counselor, social worker, etc.) who can advise you as to the best approach to deal with your particular situation.

Rewriting Your Story

Another helpful approach to dealing with the past is referred to as "rewriting your story." We tend to think about our lives in terms of stories or narratives, and these stories include, most importantly, the role we played in the events that transpired—hero or victim, loved or unworthy, competent or inadequate. It is also true that our narratives do not necessarily portray history accurately. In fact, many of our memories contain distortions of events—viewing things more positively or negatively than were actually the case—and we have a tendency to idealize the positive and exaggerate the negative.

Unfortunately, for various reasons, we come away from negative experiences, especially childhood experiences, viewing ourselves in demeaning and critical ways, perhaps even blaming ourselves for the upsetting and painful events from the past. For example, a boy whose parents divorced when he was five years old might feel responsible and blame himself for his parents' marital difficulties. Or a girl who was verbally abused by her mother might feel bad about herself because she believes that her mother would not have done that unless she was somehow deserving of that kind of treatment.

An adult man was traumatized at eight years old when his mother died of cancer. For many years thereafter, he believed that her death somehow had to do with him because he was not obedient enough as a child. Another man was self-conscious all through high school and believed that girls were not interested in him because of his problem with acne. At a class reunion many years later, he was talking to a woman who was a member of his class and knew him quite well. When he told her that he suffered from low-self-esteem in high school and believed girls did not like him because of his acne, she replied, "What acne?" What seemed like a huge problem to him in his teenage years may have gone completely unnoticed by his high school friends.

"Rewriting your story" can be a powerful tool for combating the critical, self-blaming, and unrealistic perspectives that you carry from your past. What it does *not* involve is *making up* a new story or changing the facts regarding what happened. "Rewriting your story" does suggest looking at what transpired through a different lens, and reframing the experience. The facts stay the same, but your role in the event is "rewritten," taking a more empathic and balanced view. For example, instead of viewing yourself as bad, weak, stupid, selfish or incompetent, try to view yourself and your reactions in a more understanding and reasonable way. The goal is to develop more accurate and realistic explanations of your life experiences and a more compassionate approach to your role in those circumstances.

Consider Jan, a woman who was critical and demeaning of herself whenever she became impatient with her children and yelled at them. Looking back at her past, she recalled that her mother yelled and screamed at her when she was a child, thereby modeling the behavior that she currently detested and mercilessly punished herself for exhibiting. With the help of a good friend, she was able to see how her mother's example of anger affected her responses to her own children which, in turn, caused her to feel bad about herself. She was then able to take a more empathetic stance with herself, realizing that her style of dealing with her children was based on her experience growing up and was not happening because she was inherently a mean person or a bad mother. Armed with a more compassionate and accepting view of herself and her past, she was able to honestly look at how she was interacting with her children and take steps to treat them with more understanding and patience. When she did overreact or yell, she experienced less shame and self-criticism, which increased her sense of hope, confidence, and resolve to do better.

As we seek to understand our past behaviors through the lens of compassion, we realize that there are usually explanations for our behavior, based on our life circumstances and experiences that are more realistic and helpful than the negative views we have constructed about ourselves. Sometimes we act in certain ways because that is what we have seen or what others have done to us, as in the above example. There are also external events that can affect our behavior, such as the case of an adolescent boy becoming verbally denigrating to his siblings as a result of the stress in the family generated by his parents' marital conflicts.

As we mature, we also develop survival strategies that help us to cope with difficult life situations. Unfortunately, these strategies, while once useful, can get in the way of coping with current challenges and relationships effectively. For example, consider the case of a man who struggles in his marriage because he has great difficulty dealing with any kind of emotional closeness with his wife. He came from a family where emotions were viewed as weak and unnecessary. His parents, because of their own struggles, were emotionally unavailable to their children. His survival strategy in that situation was to deny any emotional needs and to keep a more detached interpersonal stance. While this helped him to survive emotionally as he was growing up, later in life it created significant problems in his marital relationship.

Lastly, our behavior may sometimes be the result of the vicissitudes of simply being human and fallible. We occasionally make bad decisions, use poor judgment, act impulsively, make mistakes, and commit sins. A colleague of ours recalled,

I knew a man who developed an addiction to pornography over a period of years that had detrimental effects on his family relationships, work productivity, and spirituality. Finally, when his addiction led to behavior that was illegal, he was forced to confront his problem and seek treatment. Eventually, he was successful at curbing the addictive behavior and repairing some of the damage but continued to punish himself for what he had done, viewing himself as weak and selfish. Furthermore, he was unable to accept his human frailties and vulnerabilities. This mode of dealing with his weaknesses and struggles impaired his ability to forgive himself and move forward with his life.

It should be noted that when we speak of looking at yourself and your past with kindness, compassion, and understanding, we are not suggesting that you avoid taking responsibility for your behavior or seek to put the blame on others. Eventually, we all have to accept our contribution to our difficulties, be responsible adults, and proactively seek to repair and overcome what has happened. However, if you treat yourself with contempt and criticism for your past mistakes and weaknesses, it is much more difficult to have an honest and realistic perspective about your past, the present, who you really are, and who you have the potential to become.

Repairing Past Relationships

As you reflect on your life, you can probably think of relationships that were once valued and meaningful but have become strained, conflictual or non-existent. The rupture of important connections is not uncommon in our society and includes relationships with siblings, parents, spouses, and friends. Whether this results from disuse, conflict, misunderstandings, or some other kind of rift, these disruptions are usually painful and can have far-reaching consequences.

One way to feel a greater sense of peace in life is to repair and restore once meaningful relationships, especially when you have played a role in their undoing. Perhaps you had a disagreement with a friend, were disloyal to a spouse, co-worker, or church member, consistently disrespectful to a parent or perpetually mean to a sibling. To get started you will first have to admit to yourself that you had some contribution to what happened and that it is time to stop ignoring the problem or placing the blame on others. You will also need to be motivated by a genuine desire to make things right and regain an important relationship.

Next, it will be necessary to reach out and reconnect, letting the other person know that it is your desire to make amends. This process includes admitting to the harm you inflicted without blaming them or anyone else and offering a heartfelt, authentic expression of remorse. It will also be important to let the other person express their feelings toward you and about what happened. This will probably not be easy, especially when you are faced with the pain, anger, and upset that person may be expressing, and will require constraint and a willingness to validate their feelings without rebutting them.

Ted remembers going through this process with his younger sister whom he did not always treat well during a certain period of his teenage years:

After communicating my desire to repair our relationship and admitting to the unkind things I remembered doing, she told me about her memories of what happened, how hurtful it was to her and how it made her feel. It was not easy to listen to what she said, but I did my best to be understanding and validating, and I expressed my sincere apology for what I had done, which she accepted. The experience was cleansing and healing for both of us and I felt a closeness and kindness toward her that was gratifying to me. It actually turned out to be the first of three similar conversations we had over a period of years, each of which contributed to our developing a much more positive and meaningful connection.

Forgiving Others

Repairing relationships with others not only requires you to admit how you may have injured them but also involves forgiving those who have hurt you. Many people harbor anger, angst, and resentment that causes them to feel angry and unhappy. Often the bitterness they feel is a result of being mistreated, hurt, betrayed, deceived, rejected, or abused. The injury may have been inflicted by a parent, sibling, relative, friend, or teacher and could have occurred one time or been continuous over many years. Whatever the cause, the ability to heal and overcome what happened requires forgiving the offender.

Forgiving others is an essential element in relieving inner turmoil, becoming aligned with God and attaining peace in life. It is also an integral part of the gospel plan of redemption, and personal forgiveness for sin is a necessity for entrance into the Lord's kingdom. At the same time, forgiving others is also required by the Lord, who stated, "I the Lord will forgive whom I will forgive, but of you it is required to forgive all men."[4]

In addition to being a requirement of the gospel, forgiveness has other benefits, including the emotional and physiological consequences of letting go of hostility, resentment, anger, and fear. For example, people who have chronic anger and harbor resentments have been shown to experience changes in blood pressure, heart rate, and immune response that puts them at higher risk for heart disease and diabetes among other things.[5] On the other hand, individuals who practice forgiveness have lower levels of anxiety, depression, and stress and experience greater feelings of well-being.[6] Those who do not forgive are also likely to eventually lose important relationships, which decreases both physical and emotional health. As Confucius said, "If you devote your life to seeking revenge, first dig two graves."

Forgiving others is usually a process, not an event, or something that happens in the moment. It begins by acknowledging the range of feelings you have about what happened, including such emotions as anger, sadness, hate, powerlessness, and humiliation. The next step is to make a conscious decision to forgive the offender and begin to let go of the desire for revenge and retribution. This can be a difficult step because it may seem unfair or go against your sense of justice to allow someone go unpunished for their crime. While your anger and desire for justice can help motivate you to take action to protect yourself or confront a person who has hurt you, eventually you will need to come to the realization that there is more value in forgiving and healing than staying angry. Furthermore, forgiveness is ultimately a decision, not a capitulation.

An often overlooked, but invaluable part of getting past the desire for retribution is developing understanding and compassion for the offender. This is often a difficult thing to do, especially when you have been hurt and your natural inclination is to focus on what the other person did to you. Looking at the offender with compassion involves taking the perspective that he or she is probably acting in accordance with their own life experience, along with current stresses and circumstances, and is, like the rest of us, a flawed human being who struggles with their own emotional and spiritual issues. From this vantage point the offender's behavior may be seen, not as an act of a bad or malicious person who is undeserving of understanding, but as the misguided behavior of a child of God who may be behaving badly but who has the potential to act much better than they are now or have acted in the past.

Moving forward with forgiveness will usually require giving up the idea that others need to change or apologize to be deserving of forgiveness, and accepting that some things that happen in life are not fair or good. At the same time, forgiveness does not mean condoning bad behavior or letting the offender off without consequences. It is a matter of letting go of the desire for retribution and accepting that, ultimately, it is necessary to let God be the judge of the person who has hurt or offended you. It is also helpful to keep in mind that you do not have to like the person who offended you or feel that you have to interact with them. In some cases, as in dealing with a toxic person, it is prudent to protect yourself and limit any interpersonal contact.

In some instances you might be tempted to refuse to forgive someone for their offense. This might be the result of the egregious nature of the offense, or it could be an effort to feel a sense of power or moral superiority over those who injured you. In the latter case, your injury can be like a flag waving in the air, trumpeting the suffering you have endured and the evils of those who wronged you. Taking this position might provide some sense of victory over the offender but ultimately brings no lasting relief or healing.

An unwillingness to forgive is not only contrary to the spirit of the gospel and the commandments of the Lord, but is also a refusal to allow the atonement of Jesus Christ to work in the lives of others. As the Savior taught the Nephites regarding those who have committed sins: "ye shall not cast him out of your synagogues, or your places of worship, for unto such shall ye continue to minister; for ye know not but what they will return and repent, and come unto me with full purpose of heart, and I shall heal them."[7]

It can seem almost impossible to forgive someone who has caused great hurt in your life. It may feel like it is beyond your capacity to do it. At these times it is vital to remember that forgiveness is a process which is usually gradual and only completed over a long period of time. There are, however, circumstances where the capacity to forgive others can come quickly and unexpectedly, perhaps after laboring over it for an extended period.

Consider the following case example: We know a woman, whom we will call Julie, who was physically and verbally abused by her mother during her growing up years. Later in her life her mother was diagnosed with terminal cancer, and Julie traveled to another state to visit her while she was in the hospital. Unfortunately, her mother was frustrated and angry with her situation and was, once again, verbally abusive. This was upsetting to Julie and caused her to experience many of the same feelings of hurt, anger, and resentment toward her mother that she had struggled with earlier in her life. As she prayed to the Lord for help in dealing with her mother and her feelings, she had the strong impression that she needed to forgive her. This came as a shock, and she honestly did not believe she had the ability or strength to do it. All she could do was pour out her heart to God telling him that he would have to take away the pain and hatred she felt toward her mother because she was not able to do it. And that is exactly what happened. In that prayerful moment, all the anger and resentment evaporated, completely taken away, and for the first time she was able to let go of the burden of all the negative feelings she had and replaced them with tolerance and understanding. This resulted in a much longed for sense of inner peace about her relationship with her mother.

The Savior's admonition to his disciples to "Love your enemies, bless them that curse you, do good to them that hate you, and pray for them which despitefully use you, and persecute you"[8] may be exactly opposite of what you feel like doing, but paradoxically, if followed, it can lead to a changed attitude toward those who have hurt or mistreated you and open the way to forgiving and healing.

Our goal is not just to forgive others in specific instances when they have trespassed against us but to develop a forgiving nature, an attitude of forgiveness, much like our Heavenly Father.[9] This helps us to be slow to take offense and to quickly relieve ourselves of animosity toward others who hurt or wrong us along with the burden of festering resentments and grudges.

Repentance and Change

Just as it is important for us to forgive others, it is equally important that we consistently engage in the repentance process ourselves, seeking forgiveness for sins and reconciling ourselves to God. If we view sin as a movement away from God, then repentance can be understood as movement toward God and progress toward becoming more like him. As President Russell M. Nelson has clearly taught, "Thus, when Jesus asks you and me to 'repent,' He is inviting us to change our mind, our knowledge, our spirit—even the way we breathe. He is asking us to change the way we love, think, serve, spend our time, treat our wives, teach our children, and even care for our bodies."[10]

Each week we have the opportunity to partake of the sacrament and, if we repent, to experience the cleansing and renewing power of the Holy Ghost through the Atonement of Jesus Christ. Our reliance on the Atonement of Christ is the greatest resource we have for overcoming and making peace with the past. The redeeming power of the Atonement gives us the opportunity to learn from our mistakes without being punished for them.[11] We, therefore, can have the confidence that whatever sins and mistakes we have made in past can be overcome and put behind us, and the Lord will "remember them no more"[12] if we approach him with a "broken heart and a contrite spirit"[13] and truly repent.

In addition, the enabling and strengthening power of the Atonement of Christ can help us come to terms with our weaknesses and human frailties that sometimes cause us to sin and often rack us with feelings of inadequacy, shame, or worthlessness. We can have confidence that our weaknesses—areas of incompetency, failures, and self-doubts—can eventually be turned to strengths if we are humble and exercise faith in Christ.[14] If we continue on that course we have the promise that eventually "we shall be like him." [15]

Forgiving Ourselves

If we truly believe that the Lord will forgive us for our sins and strengthen us in our weaknesses, then we also need to learn how to forgive ourselves for our mistakes, mishaps and for being imperfect. Forgiving ourselves can be the most difficult part of repentance and change because we sometimes hold ourselves to a standard that does not make room for being human, for making bad choices, for not doing what we know we should do, and for acting beneath our potential. When we do not forgive ourselves for these things, we are also negating the power of the Atonement of Jesus Christ in a way that sounds like, "it can work for everyone but me." Commenting on this, Elder Jeffrey R. Holland has said,

> There is something in us, at least in too many of us, that particularly fails to forgive and forget earlier mistakes in life—either mistakes we ourselves have made or the mistakes

of others. That is not good. It is not Christian. It stands in terrible opposition to the grandeur and majesty of the Atonement of Christ. To be tied to earlier mistakes—our own or other people's—is the worst kind of wallowing in the past from which we are called to cease and desist.[16]

To forgive yourself requires you to develop a spirit of compassion and kindness for your humanness—your weaknesses, tendency to fall short, and proclivities to make mistakes. One way to do this is, when you make a mistake, think about how a good friend, someone who knows and cares about you, would react to what happened. A good friend would probably be honest with you about what you did but would also be kind and understanding, taking into consideration why it happened and the circumstances involved. They would likely be less interested in criticism and more focused on how they could help you.

Perhaps the good friend you thought of was Jesus Christ. He is a good friend to each of us and we could feel confident that his approach would include the kind of compassion he demonstrated in his well-known conversation with the woman who had been caught committing adultery. After her accusers had left the scene, Jesus asked her, "Woman, where are those thine accusers? hath no man condemned thee?" Following her reply, he reassuringly said, "Neither do I condemn thee: go, and sin no more."[17] So much for judging and accusing ourselves. Certainly, honest self-evaluation, guilt and remorse are important elements in the repentance process, but excessive self-criticism and self-punishment and harsh, unforgiving attitudes toward self are not the Lord's way and are not necessary or helpful.

One perspective that can be helpful as we try to forgive ourselves is realizing that forgiving ourselves does not necessarily mean forgetting about the sin, but it does mean that we can view ourselves as a person who is different from the one who committed the sin. In this regard, Elder Tad R. Callister taught: "when we repent, we are 'born of God.' We become, as the scriptures say, 'new creatures' in Christ. With perfect honesty we can now say, 'I am not the man or woman who committed those past sins. I am a new and transformed being.'"[18]

The hurts, injuries, losses, mistakes, and regrets of the past, when acknowledged, understood, and addressed from a compassionate and realistic perspective, can open the door to healing and growth. This, in turn, leads to a greater capacity to more fully live in and enjoy the present and look with faith to the future. When the present is fulfilling and includes successful experiences, the past becomes less important and influential and the future is more welcoming and inviting. This seems to be what the Apostle Paul meant when he said, "This one thing I do, forgetting those things which are behind, and reaching forth unto those things which are before, I press toward the mark for the prize of the high calling of God in Christ Jesus."[19]

References to Chapter 2

1   George Santayana, *The Life of Reason: Reason in Common Sense*, (New York: C. Scribner's Sons, 1905), 284.

2   John 14:26

3   John 14:26

4   D&C 64:10

5   "Forgiveness: Your Health Depends on it," Johns Hopkins Medicine, www. johnshopkinsmedicine.org.

6   Kristen Weir, "Forgiveness Can Improve Mental and Physical Health," *Monitor on Psychology*, January 2017, 30.

7   3 Nephi 18:32

8   Matthew 5:44

9   Joseph Smith, "The Character of God," *Lectures on Faith*, Lecture 3, 20.

10 Russell M. Nelson, "We Can Do Better and Be Better," *Ensign*, May 2019.

11 Bruce C. Hafen, "The Atonement: All for All," *Ensign*, May 2004.

12 D&C 58:42

13 3 Nephi 9:20

14 See Ether 12:27

15 Moroni 7:48

16 Jeffrey R. Holland, "Remember Lot's Wife: Faith is For the Future," *BYU Speeches*, January 13, 2009.

17 John 8:10–11

18 Tad R. Callister, "The Atonement of Jesus Christ," *Ensign*, May 2019.

19 Philippians 3:13–14

Chapter 3

DEVELOPING A SPIRIT
OF OPTIMISM

*The spirit of the gospel is optimistic; It trusts in
God and looks on the bright side of things.*

—Elder Orson F. Whitney [1]

HAVE YOU EVER been around someone who is negative, critical, or pessimistic for an extended period of time? It wears you down, doesn't it? Sometimes it can become downright depressing just being around such individuals. Anyone can be negative or critical. Being a "sourpuss" does not require any talent, effort, or thinking. The secret to happiness in life is to be able to find the good in other individuals and in our own circumstances. Perhaps all of us need to surround ourselves with more individuals who are optimistic about the future and who can see the good in others.

Mark related the following:

When I served as a bishop, I was protective of our youth. This meaning that when it came to selecting youth leaders, our bishopric was always focused on praying over men and women who had "positive energy"—those who were happy, enthusiastic, optimistic, and of course, who had strong testimonies of the gospel of Jesus Christ. I did not want any of our leaders poisoning our youth, leading them down a pathway of negativity or criticism, or causing them to one day turn against the Church because they might find fault in the leaders. Perhaps as adults, we could also surround ourselves with such wonderful individuals.

Here is another observation. I (Mark) have taught for over ten years at Brigham Young University. One of the courses I teach in our religion department is called, "The Living Prophets." The essence of the course is to study the lives of our modern-day Apostles and Prophets and their teachings. One common thread I have noticed in all fifteen of those men is a spirit of faith, hope, and optimism. Each one of them is a believer in "good things to come." Each one of them believes that the future is as bright as our faith.[2]

Each of us can be inspired by our Apostles and Prophets—their faith, their hope, and their confidence in the future. For example, at a recent General Conference, Elder Jeffrey R. Holland, despite the horrific conditions of our world, said, "I testify that the future is going to be as miracle-filled and bountifully blessed as the past has been. We have every reason to hope for blessings even greater than those we have already received because this is the world of Almighty God, this is the Church of continuing revelation, this is the gospel of Christ's unlimited grace and benevolence."[3]

Doctrinal Underpinnings of Optimism

Surrounding ourselves with positive energy is a key to our mental health, and having a spirit of optimism and hope is crucial to our spiritual well-being. Our Latter-day Saint theology teaches us that we should seek for hope and happiness in this life. We know from the scriptures that "men are, that they might have joy" (2 Nephi 2:25). Our purpose on this earth, regardless of our circumstances, is to be happy, to find the good, to be positive, and to be believing. On another occasion, the Lord declared, "Wherefore, be of good cheer, and do not fear, for I the Lord am with you, and will stand by you" (Doctrine & Covenants 68:6).

It is becoming increasingly difficult for some to find happiness in this life, which is completely understandable. We are bombarded with twenty-four-hour news cycles that do nothing other than spread doom, gloom, fear, and hopelessness. Presently, this world is quite disheartening to say the least. There are wars, terrorism, riots, natural disasters, economic concerns and other crucial social problems of the day. This is not even to mention the personal problems that many families face with death, disease, financial reversals, marriage troubles, wayward children, and for some, a crisis in faith.

Despite these challenges, we can still be positive and optimistic. Do you remember this phrase from the Book of Mormon? "But behold, there never was a happier time among the people of Nephi, since the days of Nephi, than in the days of Moroni" (Alma 50:23). When was this statement made? Was it in 4 Nephi, right after Jesus came? Could it have been in 3 Nephi, when Christ appeared to his people? No. None of the above! This statement was made right in the middle of the war chapters. That's right—right in the middle of one of the most turbulent times in Nephite history. But these people had everything they needed! They had their families; they had their faith; and they were being led by a righteous prophet in Moroni. In essence, we have these same blessings today.

President Gordon B. Hinckley was a modern-day Prophet of great faith, hope, and optimism. He taught, "I see so many people . . . who seem never to see the sunshine, but who constantly walk with storms under cloudy skies. Cultivate an attitude of happiness. Cultivate a spirit of optimism. Walk with faith, rejoicing in the beauties of nature, in the goodness of those you love, in the testimony which you carry in your heart concerning things divine."[4]

President Boyd K. Packer once declared, "when I think of the future, I am overwhelmed with a feeling of positive optimism."[5]

Voicing a similar view. Elder Richard G. Scott stated,

Personally, I am enthusiastic about the future. You can be too. You are living in the most exciting period of time in history. Many reasons could be cited for that optimism. Yet your greatest source of hope and assurance is that you have the fullness of the teachings of the Master. They will show you how to live a good life. You can receive ordinances and covenants that when righteously lived assure true happiness and significant attainment.[6]

Likewise, Bishop Richard C. Edgley, who served in the presiding bishopric of the church several years ago, told the students at Brigham Young University,

> Yes indeed, we do live in a troubled and challenging world. But we live in one of the greatest periods of time in all the history of the entire world. It is a time that I believe every prophet since the creation of the earth prophesied of and looked forward to. We have every reason to be optimistic and full of hope—hope for this life, hope for our children, and hope for the eternities to come. And so I say never, never let Satan's power of belittlement, discouragement, or disillusionment direct your lives.[7]

Many years ago, President Howard W. Hunter also spoke to the students at Brigham Young University. He said,

> I am here tonight to tell you that despair, doom, and discouragement are not an acceptable view of life for a Latter-day Saint. . . . I am just a couple of years older than most of you, and in those few extra months I have seen a bit more of life than you have. I want you to know that there have always been some difficulties in mortal life and there always will be. But knowing what we know, and living as we are supposed to live, there really is no place, no excuse, for pessimism and despair.[8]

Many other statements could be cited, but we are confident that you are probably "catching the drift" of what our apostles and prophets have written and stated about faith, hope, and optimism. In a world of craziness and uncertainly, we can exercise our agency and choose to be positive. The thirteenth article of faith states that "we follow the admonition of Paul—We believe all things, we hope all things, we have endured many things, and hope to be able to endure all things. If there is anything virtuous, lovely, or of good report or praiseworthy, we seek after these things." We can fill our lives with the positive; we should attempt to eliminate from our lives negative, draining influences. We can seek to be around those with positive light, love, and energy. And of course, we can radiate all of these good things to those around us.

Research on Optimism

Not only have modern prophets shared their feelings about the blessings of optimism. Social science researchers have also documented incredible benefits about taking a more positive approach to life. For example, optimism has been related to positive physical health. In one study, 309 middle-aged patients completed a pre-operative physical exam, as well as a psychological evaluation to measure optimism. Six months after their coronary bypass surgery, "optimists were only half as likely as pessimists to require re-hospitalization."[9] Other research studies have shown that those who are optimistic have lower blood pressure, better heart health, and better overall health. Another study showed that those who are optimistic live longer than their pessimistic peers.[10]

In another study, optimism was operationalized using the *Minnesota Multiphasic Personality Inventory* (MMPI). The researchers found that for every 10 point increase on the individual's optimism score, their risk of death decreased by 19 percent.[11] Other studies have documented that optimism can help people survive cancer[12] and can protect individuals from chronic illnesses.[13] Optimists seem to be healthier, and live longer than pessimists.

Another study conducted in the United States looked at almost 7,000 students who entered the University of North Carolina in the mid-1960s. During the next forty years, 476 people died from a variety of causes—cancer being the most common. All in all, pessimism took a substantial toll; the most pessimistic individuals had a 42 percent higher rate of death than the most optimistic.[14]

From a mental health perspective, optimism wins again. Optimism has been linked to better responses to difficult situations.[15] Moreover, optimism is directly correlated with life satisfaction and self-esteem.[16] Optimists also appear to recover from disappointments more quickly by focusing on positive outcomes and ignoring negative ones.[17]

Learned Optimism

Optimism is a wonderful quality that can have a valuable impact on shaping our perspectives about the future. It is essentially the expectation that the future is bright, and that we can expect good things to come. This view is based on not only the expectation that good things will happen, but also that setbacks and challenges can be faced and overcome.

People who are optimistic see problems as a normal part of life, are confident in their ability to face them, and view them as challenges and opportunities that can bring about positive changes. Pessimists, on the other hand, hold the expectation that bad things will certainly happen, are doubtful about their ability to deal with problems, and view them as something to be avoided. Winston Churchill succinctly summed it up when he said, "A pessimist sees the difficulty in every opportunity; an optimist sees the opportunity in every difficulty."[18]

Dr. Martin Seligman, a prominent psychologist and a major proponent of positive thinking, explained: "Life inflicts the same setbacks and tragedies on the optimist as on the pessimist, but the optimist weathers them better. As we have seen, the optimist bounces back from defeat, and, with his life somewhat poorer, he picks up and starts again. The pessimist gives up and falls into depression. Because of his resilience, the optimist achieves more at work, at school, and on the playing field. . . . Americans want optimists to lead them."[19]

There is no doubt that optimism is a desirable personal quality, and the good news is that being optimistic is not just reserved for those who happen to come from a good gene pool or who grew up with supportive, high functioning parents. It is something that can be learned! Now back to Dr. Martin Seligman. He and his colleagues at the University of Pennsylvania have studied optimism and have written extensively about how it can be developed.[20] Seligman views optimism in terms of how we explain negative events or how we think about the causes and the impact of adversity and setbacks. Specifically, negative events are viewed as:

- Temporary—"this won't last forever"
- Limited in scope—"my life isn't over" and "it isn't a catastrophe"
- Manageable—"this is changeable" and "I can overcome what happened"

Optimistic people are also realistic about how much responsibility they have for what occurs in their lives. They are not overly self-blaming or overly blaming of others—"I shouldn't have lost my cool in the meeting, but all of us seemed to be upset and over-reacting."

The following is an example of how optimism/pessimism might look in a marital conflict:

- *Pessimist:* "I had another fight with my wife. We started talking about finances and she blew up (blaming wife for problem). It was the worst (problem is viewed as huge). I don't think we will ever be able to talk about it (problem viewed as permanent) or work it out (problem viewed as unchangeable).
- *Optimist:* I had another fight with my wife. We both got pretty tense when we started talking about money (balanced level of responsibility). I think this is something we can get past (problem viewed limited and temporary) if we keep talking about it and working on finding solutions (problem viewed as changeable).

Developing the ability to look at problems through the lens of optimism—as temporary, limited in scope and changeable—can certainly increase one's sense of confidence about facing whatever the future might hold. Acquiring this perspective, like most skills, requires intentional effort and practice over time and in many different situations. Fortunately, most of us have plenty of situations that arise in our lives that will facilitate this kind of practice.

Furthermore, it is important to keep in mind that there is a difference between *blind* and *realistic* optimism. Blind optimism is based on unrealistic views of our abilities and our level of control and can lead to over-confidence, poor judgment, and a reduction in effort. Examples of such confidence would be a teenager who feels he will be safe driving fast on a dark, curvy road or woman who believes she can love her fiancé out of his bad habits.

Realistic optimism, on the other hand, involves accepting limitations and acknowledging a lack of control over some things, yet with the expectation of being able to influence outcomes. An example would be a parent who tries to instill good study habits in her daughter and has optimistic expectations about her daughter's academic performance, but realizes she can't control the grades her daughter gets in college.

Another example of realistic optimism occurred when President Gordon B. Hinckley accepted an invitation to be interviewed by Mike Wallace on the CBS television news program, *60 Minutes*, which was aired April 7, 1996. In describing this experience in general conference just before the interview was aired, our former Prophet stated,

> Months ago I was invited to be interviewed by Mike Wallace, a tough senior reporter for the CBS 60 Minutes program, which is broadcast across America to more than 20 million listeners each week. I recognized that if I were to appear, critics and detractors of the Church would also be invited to participate. I knew we could not expect that the program would be entirely positive for us.
>
> On the other hand, I felt that it offered the opportunity to present some affirmative aspects of our culture and message to many millions of people. I concluded that it was better to lean into the stiff wind of opportunity than to simply hunker down and do nothing. It has been an interesting experience. . . . We have no idea what the outcome will be—that is, I don't. We will discover this this evening when it is aired in this valley. If it turns out to be favorable, I will be grateful. Otherwise, I pledge I'll never get my foot in that kind of trap again.[21]

President Hinckley's comments reflected his optimism that something good would come out of the interview, as well as an acknowledgment there was some risk involved. His words also revealed his view that even if the interview did not turn out favorably, it was still worth taking the risk to do it. Moreover, he seemed to imply in his statement that even if the outcome of the interview was not all positive and could be disappointing, it would not be a major setback for the church. Additionally, he indicated that he would accept responsibility for what happened and not repeat it if it was an unfavorable venture.

Becoming More Optimistic

As with improving in endeavors, such as skiing, playing a musical instrument, or even learning a language, becoming more optimistic will take practice and effort. However, anyone with the desire can learn to be more positive and confident in the future. Here are several suggestions for you to consider.

1. Create or collect some positive statements and review them daily. Repetition is a way to reprogram the way your brain works. Statements such as your own positive affirmations, declarations from living prophets, scriptures, and quotations from heroes of the past or other historical figures can be most helpful. For example, President James E. Faust, formerly of the First Presidency, said, "Let us not take counsel from our fears. May we remember always to be of good cheer, put our faith in God, and live worthy for Him to direct us."[22] Or how about this one, again, from former United States President Calvin Coolidge: "If you see ten troubles coming down the road, you can be sure that nine will run into the ditch before they reach you."[23] Write statements such as these on a 3 x 5 card and review them throughout the day. Many of these can be found on google and other search engines.

2. Learn to focus on the positives and ignore the negatives. In a given day, most of the things that happen to us are usually positive. Our children had a good day at school; we made it to work safely and were semi-productive; we have money in our checking account and gas in the tank of our mini-van; and we will have food on our tables tonight. Once again, most of the things that happen to us—usually—are positive. However, if one negative incident occurs during our day, such as losing our car keys, getting a flat tire, or perhaps becoming sick, many of us behave as if the entire world is falling apart. Sure,

bad things are going to happen to us, but we should remember that, if we were to keep track of our daily activities, we would discover that most of the things that happen to us are positive.

3. Believe in Good things. In the Book of Mormon, we are reminded to "Believe in God; believe that He is, and that he created all things, both in heaven and in earth; believe that he has all wisdom, and all power, both in heaven and in earth; believe that man doth not comprehend all the things which the Lord can comprehend" (Mosiah 4:9). Indeed, God does live, he created everything on this earth, and he has all wisdom and power! Christian author, Max Lucado wrote, "Lift up your eyes. Don't get lost in your troubles. Dare to believe that good things will happen. . . . Are you troubled, restless, sleepless? Then rejoice in the Lord's sovereignty. I dare you—I double dog dare you—to expose your worries to an hour of worship. Your concerns will melt like ice on a July sidewalk. Anxiety passes as trust increases."[24]

4. Keep a gratitude journal. In the Book of Philippians, we read, "Do not be anxious about anything, but in every situation, by prayer and petition, with thanksgiving, present your requests to God. And the peace of God, which transcends all understanding, will guard your hearts and your minds in Christ Jesus" (Philippians 4:6–7; NIV version). We love the counsel: "Do not be anxious," but to also be "thankful." Gratitude is an incredible panacea for anxiety and stress. Once again, Max Lucado, wrote: "As you look at your blessings, take note of what happens. Anxiety grabs his bags and slips out the back door. Worry refuses to share the heart with gratitude. One heartfelt thank-you will suck the oxygen out of worry's world. So say it often. Focus more on what you do have and less on what you don't."[25] Remember the hymn we love to sing: "Count your many blessings; name them one by one, and it will surprise you what the Lord has done."[26] At the end of each day, sit down and write down several things you are grateful for. You will find great peace, and you will see the Lord's hand in your life as you engage in this wonderful endeavor.

5. Challenge every negative thought that comes into your mind. Just as many of us were taught in our adolescence to control and manage our impure thoughts, the same rules apply with stress and anxiety. We must control our thoughts—we should not let those thoughts control us. No one can afford to let negative, pessimistic thoughts take root in their minds, grow, and expand. When an undesirable thought enters your mind, cast it out immediately and replace it with something positive, optimistic, or hopeful. If you cannot do that, then at least imagine yourself on a remote island in the South Pacific—that works almost every time. On a serious note, remember what Jesus taught, "Look unto me in every thought; doubt not, fear not" (Doctrine and Covenants 6:36). President Boyd K. Packer once counseled, "If you can fill your mind with clean, constructive thoughts, then there will be no room for these persistent imps, and they will leave."[27] Fill your mind with positive music, positive thoughts, and constructive ideas. Look for the positive in every situation.

6. Turn off the news and detach from social media. When we make this suggestion, we realize that we must be careful. Of course, you should be informed and know what is going on in the world. However, we have actually been in homes where news programs are on television all day long. In fact, we know another person who actually listens to political talk radio practically from morning until night. The minute you turn on the news, for example, you will be bombarded with negativity and the depressing conditions of the world around us. Remember, to be emotionally healthy, we all need balance in our lives, and certainly moderation. There is a reason that our Prophet, President Russell M. Nelson invited the youth, and even the women of the Church, to participate in a seven-day social media fast.[28] For those who engaged in that sacrifice, they reported unbelievable results regarding their positive moods and how often they felt the spirit in their lives. Perhaps all of us should take the Prophet's invitation and disengage from media more often.

7. Recognize what you can and what you cannot control. Too much of what goes on in this life is out of our jurisdiction, and therefore, out of our control. We will be much more optimistic if we focus on our own "ten acres," and leave the rest of the worries in the world to those who made those messes in the first place. Besides, there is nothing we can do about natural disasters, the economy, or wars in other nations. However, there are plenty of things that we can focus on within the realm of our own responsibilities. We can be more optimistic if we focus on those things that we have some control over.

8. Look for the good in everyone. Everyone loves someone who has a positive attitude and who radiates positive energy. Find a way to be that person for others. Always have a smile on your face and a positive comment. Compliment others for the good that they do. Send notes, texts, and emails to those in your life who always seem to bless you. Congratulate others on their accomplishments and achievements. Tell people—especially youth—that you are proud of them. Look for the good in others and ignore the bad. Not only will you be happier, but so will those with whom you interact.

Remember, being an optimist is a choice. In fact, if you are pessimistic, that is because you have made the choice to react that way to the world around you. Now—today—is a wonderful opportunity to change. Anyone can be negative—that is too easy. A challenge and an opportunity in this life is to become a true-blooded optimist. Remember, we are here on this earth to act, and "not to be acted upon" (2 Nephi 2:14, 16, 26). This world, and this Church, needs more optimists—we have plenty of pessimists—perhaps too many. Now is the time to act with hope faith, courage, and conviction.

References to Chapter 3

1   Orson F. Whitney, *Conference Report*, April 1917, 43.

2   Thomas S. Monson, "Be of Good Cheer," *Ensign*, May 2009.

3   Jeffrey R. Holland, "A Perfect Brightness of Hope," *Ensign*, May 2020.

4   Gordon B. Hinckley, "If Thou Art Faithful," *Ensign*, November 1984, 92.

5   Boyd K. Packer, "On Zion's Hill," *Ensign*, November 2006, 23.

6   Richard G. Scott, "The Power of Righteousness," *Ensign,* November 1998, 5.

7   Richard C. Edgley, "Faith, Hope, and You," BYU Speeches, 4 November 2008.

8   Howard W. Hunter, "An Anchor to the Souls of Men," *Brigham Young University 1992–1993 Speeches*, 7 February 1993, 1–2.

9   "Optimism and Your Health," Harvard Health Publishing, Harvard Medical School, May 2008, https://www.health.harvard.edu/heart-health/optimism-and-your-health.

10 Lewina O. Lee, Peter James, Emily S. Zevon, Eric S. Kim, Claudia Trudel-Fitzgerald, Avron Spiro III, Francine Grodstein, and Laura D. Kubzansky, "Optimism is Associated with Exceptional Longevity in 2 Epidemiologic Cohorts or Men and Women," *Proceedings of the National Academy of Sciences* (26 August 2019). DOI: 10.1073/pnas.1900712116.

11 Maruta T, Colligan RC, Malinchoc M, Offord KP. "Optimists vs pessimists: survival rate among medical patients over a 30–year period." *Mayo Clin Proc.* 2000 Feb;75(2):140–3. doi: 10.4065/75.2.140. Erratum in: Mayo Clin Proc 2000 Mar;75(3):318. PMID: 10683651.

12 I. Schou, O. Ekeberg, & C.M. Ruland, "The mediating role of appraisal and coping in the relationship between optimism-pessimism and quality of life," *Psycho-Oncology: Journal of the Psychological, Social, and Behavioral Dimensions of Cancer,* 14, 9(2005), 697–791.

13 Matthews KA, Räikkönen K, Sutton-Tyrrell K, Kuller LH, "Optimistic attitudes protect against progression of carotid atherosclerosis in healthy middle-aged women," *Psychosom Med*, 2004 Sep-Oct;66 (5):640–4. doi: 10.1097/01.psy.0000139999.99756.a5. PMID: 15385685.

14 "Optimism and Your Health," Harvard Health Publishing, Harvard Medical School, May 2008, https://www.health.harvard.edu/heart-health/optimism-and-your-health.

15 I. Brissette, M. Scheier, and C. Carver, "The Role of Optimism in Social Network Development, Coping, and Psychological Adjustment During a Life Transition," *Journal of Personality and Social Psychology*, 82, 1(2002), 102–111.

16 R.E. Lucas, E. Diener, & E. Suh, "Discriminant Validity of Well-being Measures," *Journal of Personality and Social Psychology,* 71 (3) (1996), 616–628. https://doi.org/10.1037/0022-3514.71.3.616

17   See https://www.pursuit-of-happiness.org/science-of-happiness/positive-thin
      king/?gclid=Cj0KCQjwvvj5BRDkARIsAGD9vlKXhYC_ZUHS9Gn3Z6-
      P0kdhjMvnjmamoYfUX9ekHye-6XgnDWkZIuoaAnCTEALw_wcB

18   See www.goalcast.com/2017/06/20/
      top-24-winston-churchill-quotes-to-inspire-you-to-never-surrender/

19   Martin E.P. Seligman, *Learned Optimism: How to Change Your Mind and
      Your Life,*" (New York: Vintage Books, 2006), 207.

20   Seligman.

21   Gordon B. Hinckley, "Remember . . . Thy Church, O Lord," *Ensign,* May
      1996.

22   James E. Faust, "Be Not Afraid," *Ensign*, October 2002.

23   See https://www.brainyquote.com/authors/calvin-coolidge-quotes

24   Max Lucado, *Anxious For Nothing: Finding Calm in a Chaotic World*
      (Nashville, Tenn.: Thomas Nelson, 2017), 32.

25   Lucado, 96.

26   "Count Your Many Blessings," *Hymns*, no. 214.

27   Boyd K. Packer, "Worthy Music, Worthy Thoughts," *New Era*, April 2008,
      8.

28   Russell M. Nelson, "Your 7–Day Social Media Fast, *New Era*, March 2019.

Chapter 4

ACTING AND NOT BEING
ACTED UPON

*As sons and daughters of God we are agents with
the inherent capacity to act and to learn—and
not objects that primarily are acted upon.*

—Elder David A. Bednar[1]

A BASIC NEED SHARED by all humans is to feel empowered and to
be able to influence their environment and interactions with others.
This need for mastery and control begins in infancy and continues
throughout the lifespan. For example, in one study, developmental
researchers found that infants gained great pleasure from being able to
control the production of music in their cribs by pulling on a string.
When pulling the string no longer produced music they reacted to
their loss of control with anger and sadness.[2]

Much like the infants in this study, when we consistently feel pow-
erless, impinged upon by others or a lack of control over our lives, we
typically respond with feelings of anxiety and frustration. Likewise,
being unduly burdened with meeting the needs and expectations of
others, with little time and energy left over to focus on your own
interests and desires, can also lead to stress and resentment.

In contrast, experiencing a sense of control and self-direction is
associated with feelings of empowerment and well-being along with a
more positive view of oneself. In the language of the Book of Mormon,

empowerment may be analogous to the ability to *act . . . and not be acted upon*[3] described by Lehi in his discourse to his sons on agency.

Empowerment and Control

Taking control of your life can involve many things, but here we focus on the importance of self-assertion, the ability to say "no," and establishing and maintaining appropriate boundaries with others.

What does it mean to be assertive? An assertive individual is comfortable expressing needs, feelings, and opinions; is able to respectfully say no or disagree; and is not overly concerned about pleasing others. Being assertive is a healthy and helpful way of dealing with others and should be distinguished from aggressive or passive interactional styles. This distinction can be understood by considering the following example. Suppose you loaned a large sum of money to a friend (not advisable, but common) with the understanding that this person would pay you back within a specified period of time. Unfortunately, the time period for payback has elapsed, but you have not been repaid and your friend has said nothing to you about it.

A person taking a passive approach to the situation might decide that, even though they feel they should have been repaid, it is not worth the hassle and the potential conflict to talk to the friend and ask for repayment. An individual dealing with the situation in an aggressive manner might confront his friend angrily, stating something like, "I need my money and I'm tired of waiting for you to get around to paying me! Are you going to pay me back or were you hoping I would just forget about it?" The assertive person might approach his friend and say, "It has been a while since I made that loan to you. You were supposed to pay me back two weeks ago and I have not received any payment. I was wondering when I could expect to receive the payment." This approach gets directly to the point, but it is done in a respectful and non-accusatory manner.

Appropriate self-assertion implies that you are willing to stand up for yourself and act in your own best interest without disrespecting or violating the rights of others. Sometimes this means that you have to resist demands and decline requests or invitations if they are not a priority or conflict with what you deem to be important.

For example, suppose you are offered a promotion in your organization which would include a substantial increase in pay, along with an expectation that you would spend at least two days each week traveling. Your boss is putting pressure on you to accept the promotion and views it as a necessary steppingstone to your further advancement in the company. The decision you make would hopefully be based on a clear consideration of your values regarding time with family, success at work, and money. If you decide you do not want to take the job, it would be important that you felt able to act on your decision by explaining to your boss directly that you were not going to accept the position, rather than capitulating to his desires for you or passively avoiding the issue for as long as possible.

As another example, a woman who feels ignored by her husband because he is so busy with work and church responsibilities, might deal with her loneliness by withdrawing and expressing her frustration indirectly. Alternatively, she could say something to him like, "I know you are very busy with many things on your mind, but I am feeling disconnected in our marriage and would like to spend some one-on-one time with you." In this instance, she was able to communicate her feelings and needs in an assertive and respectful manner.

Developing the ability to say "no" to requests or invitations is also an important skill in feeling a sense of empowerment in your life. However, while saying "no" sounds easy, it can be difficult because the things we are being asked to do are often attractive, good, and seemingly could enhance our self-worth and provide opportunities for us to serve others. President Dallin Oakes recently counseled,

> Some time ago I gave a talk titled "Good, Better, Best." In that talk I said that "just because something is good is not a sufficient reason for doing it. The number of good things we can do far exceeds the time available to accomplish them. Some things are better than good, and these are the things that should command priority attention in our lives. . . . We have to forego some good things in order to choose others that are better or best.[4]

Moreover, when we do forgo some good things to engage in pursuits that are better or best, we often have to say "no" to individuals that we like, respect, or to whom we feel a sense of loyalty or obligation. Telling a family member, a friend at church, or a neighbor that you will not be able to fulfill a request can be hard because of concerns about disappointing, frustrating, or hurting people whom you like. You might also notice a nagging sense of feeling mean, negative, selfish, or unchristian when you do not do what others ask or expect, along with a fear that you might compromise valued relationships.

This would certainly apply to turning down a Church assignment or calling. Mark shares the following experience:

My wife, Janie, is one of the most faithful Latter-day Saints I know. She has served in every Church calling she has ever been given, including multiple primary presidencies, and young women's presidencies for the past twenty years. However, when we lived in Hyde Park, Utah many years ago, I was a full-time doctoral student, I taught practically full-time at the institute of religion, and I worked part-time at LDS Family Services two nights a week just to help make ends meet. Amidst the middle of that chaotic time in our lives, Janie was called into the young women's program. Even though we were not sure how her calling would work with me working every Wednesday night, we agreed to accept the call. It didn't take long for us to realize that was a big mistake. Every Wednesday night, Janie would head out for mutual, leaving our eleven-year-old daughter in charge of our five other children for the next two hours—with both parents away from home. This arrangement simply was not working out at home. As Janie is prone to say, "Someone needs to be with the children, 'Keeping the home fires burning.' After several months of this plan, Janie went to the bishop and asked to be released. She was sad but realized that serving in the young women's program was not right for our family at the time. Once I graduated and we left Northern Utah for Texas, the timing was much better, and Janie was in the young women's program with all of our daughters—all seven of them—for the next two decades.

It is helpful to remember that when you say "no," you are essentially affirming your selfhood, your right of agency and self-direction, and your prerogative to decide what you will and will not do. While it is wise and prudent to consider the opinions of others, especially trusted individuals, it is important that you feel free to disagree, to have your own view and to feel comfortable acting on it. Of course, things usually go better if your opinions and associated actions are well thought out and, in some cases, prayerfully considered and then expressed respectfully.

Telling others "no" is also a mark of self-respect and maturity because it involves thinking about what is best for you and what your goals, values, and desires are relative to what people want and expect from you. It is also helpful to remember that it is natural to feel some degree of guilt or discomfort whenever you assert yourself and that having those feelings is not an indication that you have done something wrong or inappropriate.

Ted remembers the following experience:

A few years ago my wife, Laura, and I decided that we were going to spend time on Friday afternoons riding bikes together. We wanted to do this for both health reasons and to spend some enjoyable quality time together in the midst of hectic everyday schedules. Each week there were many requests, needs, problems, and distractions that could have easily interfered with our time together, such as a request from a client to meet during that afternoon because it was the only time they could come, or a need at our children's school for parental involvement in an activity. In each case, we had to evaluate how important the competing need or involvement was in view of our commitment to reserve a period of time to spend together each week, and we often decided to "hold our ground" and say "no" because spending time together was a higher priority.

Please keep in mind that we are not suggesting that you say "no" to everyone, and reject every opportunity to help others. Instead, we are encouraging you to be more balanced, and to remember your own needs, and the needs of your family, when making such decisions. With Christ as the center of your life, there will be times you will feel inspired to help others, and other times when you will feel compelled to be with your family, spend time with your spouse, or to recharge your own batteries.

Another useful strategy for improving your sense of control is setting boundaries. Boundaries are guidelines, rules and limits that you create which indicate what is acceptable or unacceptable concerning the behavior of others toward you. Boundaries serve as buffers or fences, and regulate closeness, investment and commitment in relationships. Setting boundaries is essentially a statement about how involved you are going to be in any particular activity, organization or relationship and then maintaining that stance.

Boundary problems occur in families, among friends, and in work and church organizations. It is not uncommon, for example, for young married couples to feel the need to set boundaries with their parents, who usually mean well but can easily impinge on the newlyweds' need for independence, bonding, and self-direction. Likewise, parents may feel impinged upon by adult children who are having trouble "launching" into the adult world and are consistently asking for money or to live at home just a little longer. Setting reasonable boundaries in this situation, such as requiring the child to work and only allowing them to stay at home for a specified period of time, not only helps parents to avoid feeling exploited, but also can assist the child to become more proactive and responsible.

Other examples of setting appropriate boundaries include not being available to a co-worker who emotionally dumps on you, saying "*no*" to a friend who is constantly asking you to watch her children, and setting aside time for family home evening amidst a host of possible impingements and distractions from friends, work, school, and extra-curricular activities. Setting boundaries requires you to decide what your limits are, then assertively, directly, and respectfully expressing and enforcing them. It takes time and practice, and sometimes facing anxiety, to do it effectively, but it can lead to enhanced feelings of self-respect, autonomy, and self-esteem.

Controlling the Controllable

As described above, experiencing a sense of control and empowerment is important in maintaining feelings of well-being. During our developing years, most of us are taught to believe that we have significant control over what happens to us. For example, many of us believe that if we work hard, then good things will happen, and we will most likely achieve our objectives. This is referred to by psychologists as an Internal Locus of Control. Conversely, those individuals who believe they have little influence over what happens in their lives, and that outcomes are most often determined by fate, luck, destiny, and circumstances are said to have an External Locus of Control.

For most people, an internal locus of control is more appealing because it suggests that you can influence what happens and you are responsible for it—you feel more in control. Those with an external locus of control feel less responsible for what happens to them, but are more likely to experience a sense of powerlessness and a lack of control over their lives. The downside of having an internal locus of control is that you might try to control your environment and the people around you too much, which leads to excessive anxiety, stress, and frustration; wasted time and energy; damaged relationships; and a tendency to judge yourself and others too harshly.

A willingness to accept that there are some things in life that affect us, sometimes significantly, and that we have little control over them is essential to managing anxiety and enjoying a peaceful life. Examples of these types of events include losing a job because of company downsizing during a pandemic, contracting a serious illness, and having an adult child leave the church.

Most often, our efforts to exert undue control involve the people around us, such as spouses, children, friends and co-workers. Attempts to control the people closest to us may stem from our feeling that our way is the best way to do something or that if we are not in charge of what is going on, then it may not turn out the way we would like. We might also suffer from the belief that "if I am not in charge, then I am not important"; or our self-esteem might be so tied to what and how our family members are doing, especially children, that we try to control the outcomes of their endeavors. This tendency is commonly referred to as being a helicopter, snowplow, or lawnmower parent.

For example, a father might be so invested in his teenaged son doing the right things, such as participating in church, attending seminary, studying scriptures, preparing for a mission, and keeping gospel standards, that he becomes too overbearing and controlling of his son's behavior. Unknowingly, this father sows the seeds of his son's later rebellious behavior and rejection of his parent's values, including gospel teachings. Not only do parents try to control children, but spouses sometimes try to control each other out of fear of losing the other person or to combat dreaded fears of powerlessness and dependency.

Sometimes in our passion to have what we want and avoid disappointment or pain, we try to impose our will on God. We may think that if we have enough faith or are obedient enough, he will grant our wishes. This might be true at times, but what happens is always subject to the will of the Lord, which may not be consistent with our desires.

A few months ago Ted attended a priesthood meeting where one of the brethren related an experience where he and his ministering companion had been asked by a ward member with a serious illness to give him a blessing of healing. Taking the request seriously, the two ministers fasted and then administered to the sick individual promising him that he would be restored to full health. The brother relating the story went on to describe his disappointment with the outcome of the blessing. He struggled to accept that, even though he wanted the healing to occur, he did not have control over the situation. The decision about whether the man would be healed belonged to God.

At the core of our efforts to *control* is usually anxiety. It can involve any number of things, but often stems from a fear that if we are not in control, then something bad or unwanted could happen. For example, a manager in a company was very controlling with his team members because he was insecure about his own capabilities and value to the company. He was especially worried that someone on the team might outdo him by coming up with a creative idea or an innovative approach to solving a problem which would cause him to feel unimportant or irrelevant. Unfortunately, his fears of losing status in the office resulted in his forfeiting any new approaches that his team members may have been able to generate on their own.

Sidestepping the urge to control others usually involves respecting their agency, trusting their ability to exercise their agency, and believing in the value of their learning from experience. While it may be appropriate for us to try to help others at times, they are responsible for their decisions and the direction their lives take.

With the exception of young children, our anxieties, and concerns for those around us, and our desire to help, are generally best handled by focusing less on controlling them and more on being loving and available to help them. The wise counsel in in Section 121 of the Doctrine and Covenants regarding the use of priesthood authority applies here, especially the warning to avoid exercising "control or dominion or compulsion upon the souls of the children of men" and instead, seeking to influence "by persuasion, by long-suffering, by gentleness and meekness, and by love unfeigned."[5]

Finding Balance

Returning to the concept of locus of control, most people function better when they have a balance of internal and external locus of control. This approach acknowledges the reality of free agency and that what happens to us has much to do with our decisions and efforts. At the same time, we also recognize and accept that external factors, which most often are out of our control, can have a significant role in how things turn out. These factors might be described as luck, fate, destiny, timing, serendipity, and how others use their agency. With this framework in mind, we can work toward accepting our limitations, along with trying to control what is possible and appropriate to control, and turning some things we cannot control over to God. This perspective is summed up in what has become known as the serenity prayer, which states:

> *God grant me the serenity to accept the things I cannot change,*
> *Courage to change the things I can,*
> *And wisdom to know the difference.*

An experience from the life of Elder Richard G. Scott is illustrative of this type of thinking. In short order, Elder Scott had returned from his mission, married Jeanene, and commenced his work in the nuclear science field. He reported that his work was "fascinating, challenging, and absorbing." He also stated, "When combined with the natural growth experiences that come with the formation of a new family and Church assignments, I found each day filled to overflowing."[6]

Elder Scott reported that within eight months, he was being examined by a doctor for ulcers. He said that for weeks, he would come home each night with a severe headache and that only after long periods of isolation could he calm his nerves enough to get some rest and return to work the next day to begin the routine again. After struggling with what we would call stress and anxiety for months, the Lord led Elder Scott to a solution. He explained:

> I was prompted to divide mentally—and physically, where possible—all of the challenges, tasks, and assignments given to me into two categories. All of the things for which I felt responsibility but for which I could do nothing to resolve I put in a basket called "worry." Then all of those things for which I had some ability to control or resolve I put into a basket called "concern." I realized I could not resolve those things in the worry basket, so I tried hard to forget them. Later in the process I learned that putting them into the worry basket didn't mean they wouldn't be taken care of. They were resolved by those who could best handle them—and most often that was the Lord Himself. The items in the concern basket were ordered in priority. I conscientiously tried to resolve them to the best of my ability. Although I could not always fulfill all of them on schedule or to the degree of competence I desired, I did my conscientious best.
>
> As I was learning to control worry, occasionally I would feel my stomach muscles tighten and tension overcome me. I would cease whatever I was doing and, with earnest prayer for support, concentrate on relaxing and overcoming the barrier that worry produced in my life. I would mentally say, "I am not going to do another thing until I begin to control my emotions." Over a period of time those efforts were blessed by the Lord. I came to understand how He is willing to fortify, guide, and direct every phase of life. The symptoms of illness passed, and I learned how to face tasks under pressure.[7]

Elder Scott's improvement in handling stress had much to do with his ability to focus on those things that were *in his control* and to let go of those things that were *out of his control*. This solution is one that we would recommend to everyone who is struggling with anxiety or stress.

Some additional examples of a balanced perspective on control in everyday life include:

- You can give your child tools to be successful, but you cannot make her do well in school.
- You can teach your child the gospel, but you cannot determine whether he develops a testimony, serves a mission, or stays on the straight and narrow path.
- You can nag, beg, and threaten, but you cannot make your spouse change.
- You can control how much you take care of yourself, but you cannot always prevent an illness.
- You can take safety precautions, but you can't always control whether or not you will be robbed or get into a traffic accident.
- You are responsible to help others, but they are responsible for their lives.

Accepting that you may not have control over some things in your life, such as how long you will live, if you will reach the pinnacle in your career field, if your children will all stay in the church, or if you will have good health is essential to experiencing greater serenity. At the same time, it is important to remember that you do have control over what you value and how much focus and effort you put in to living your life according to those values. For example, you can control how you treat other people, whether you are honest, how much effort you put into building family relationships, and the time you spend serving the Lord and others.

In a speech given at the BYU Marriott School Convocation in 1999, former presidential candidate Mitt Romney recalled his experience sitting in his own graduation exercise and offered his thoughts about what we can and cannot control and what is important in life:

> Virtually every [graduation] speaker said something to the effect that life's success was in my control. They quoted authors like Napoleon Hill, who wrote "Think and Grow Rich." Success, they said, was up to me—how I prepared and worked, how I thought, how I created and followed a mission statement, or how I put it all together would ensure the success they knew I wanted.
>
> Now, 30 years on, I have come to a very different conclusion. The worldly success stories I have seen result from a blend of factors: yes, the choices you make and control, but also the mental equipment you were born with, more than a fair measure of serendipity, and, where He does choose to intervene, the will of our loving Father. I am not convinced that it's all up to you. Nor do I believe that if you live righteously, your stocks will rise in value, you'll get a promotion, you'll win an election, or you'll get your research published.
>
> There's an element of unpredictability, of uncertainty, of lottery, if you will, in the world that has been created for us. If you judge your life's success by the world's standards, you may be elated or you may be gravely disappointed.
>
> Now, some 20 years later, I have discovered something else about these core values, about living with integrity, about these fundamental measures of successful living: with these at our center, chance does not come into play in determining our success or failure. The ability to live with integrity with the core of our values of love, family, service, and devotion is entirely up to us. Fundamentally, this is the business of successful living.
>
> It is empowering, invigorating, and emancipating to live for the success you can control yourself, to live for your most deeply seated values and convictions.[8]

Trusting Jesus Christ

Agency and accountability are central teachings of the gospel and by using our agency to "act and not to be acted upon" we have the ability to make choices and engage in behavior that allows us to enjoy a sense of control over our lives and our destiny. This adds significantly to our feelings of peace and well-being.

At the same time, there are things in life that affect us, where we seem to have little control. Our challenge is to recognize what we *can* and *cannot* control and respond to each appropriately. When it comes to things we cannot control our task is to identify what these things are, acknowledge our limitations, accept that we cannot control them, and put our trust in the Lord Jesus Christ. It is the Savior that will assist us where we are weak, lacking, and in need of help.

When we put our trust God and try to be obedient, we can be assured that he will be at our side supporting, coaching, and loving us no matter what difficulties we face. Because of this, we can walk with hope instead of anxiety, we can have confidence in place of doubt, and contentment without undue worry. Elder Jeffrey R. Holland has passionately explained,

> If we give our heart to God, if we love the Lord Jesus Christ, if we do the best we can to live the gospel, then tomorrow— and every other day—is ultimately going to be magnificent, even if we don't always recognize it as such. Why? Because our Heavenly Father wants it to be! He wants to bless us. A rewarding, abundant, and eternal life is the very object of His merciful plan for His children! It is a plan predicated on the truth "that all things work together for good to them that love God." So keep loving. Keep trying. Keep trusting. Keep believing. Keep growing. Heaven is cheering you on today, tomorrow, and forever.[9]

With the assurance that God wants us to be happy and successful and will stand with us in our setbacks, trials and weaknesses, we can have confidence that no matter what happens, if we are faithful, things will ultimately turn out well for us. This will require not only faith in the Savior, but our willingness to act, to move forward trusting him and his promises, even if the path before us is not clear. In describing his own experience with this principle, Elder Boyd K Packer explained,

> Shortly after I was called as a General Authority, I went to Elder Harold B. Lee for counsel. He listened very carefully to my problem and suggested that I see President David O. McKay. President McKay counseled me as to the direction I should go. I was very willing to be obedient but saw no way possible for me to do as he counseled me to do.
>
> I returned to Elder Lee and told him that I saw no way to move in the direction I was counseled to go. He said, "The trouble with you is you want to see the end from the beginning." I replied that I would like to see at least a step or two ahead. Then came the lesson of a lifetime: "You must learn to walk to the edge of the light, and then a few steps into the darkness; then the light will appear and show the way before you."
>
> Then he quoted these 18 words from the Book of Mormon: dispute not because ye see not, for ye receive no witness until after the trial of your faith" [Ether 12:6].[10]

Elder David A. Bednar has also taught, *"As we act, Jesus Christ blesses us with His power. Our faith in Him grows, our confidence increases, and we can then navigate the most difficult circumstances in life knowing that we will never be alone and we will always have His help."*[11] Certainly, trusting in the Lord and acting on that trust will enable us to move forward with the expectation that, indeed, "all things will work together" (See Romans 8:28) for our good. What a wonderful foundation for a peaceful life.

References to Chapter 4

1   David A. Bednar, *Act in Doctrine*, (Salt Lake City: Deseret Book, 2012), 38.

2   M. Lewis, SM Alessandri & MW Sullivan, "Violation of expectancy, loss of control and anger expression in young infants," *Developmental Psychology*, 26(1990), 745–751.

3   2 Nephi 2:26

4   Dallin H. Oaks, "Where Will This Lead?" *Ensign*, May 2019.

5   D&C 121:37, 41

6   Richard G. Scott, "Making the Right Choices," BYU Speeches, 13 January 2002.

7   Richard G. Scott, "Making the Right Choices," BYU Speeches, 13 January 2002.

8   Mitt Romney, "Forty Years On," *BYU Magazine,* Winter 2013.

9   Jeffrey R. Holland, "Tomorrow the Lord Will Do Wonders among You," *Ensign,* May 2016.

10 Boyd K. Packer, "The Edge of the Light," *BYU Today*, March 1991.

11 See https://www.churchofjesuschrist.org/media-library/video/2016-03-0019-being-an-agent-to-act?lang=eng

Chapter 5

OVERCOMING PERFECTIONISM

We can choose to be perfect and admired or to be real and loved.

—Glennon Doyle Melton[1]

MUCH OF THE turmoil we experience in life is created as a result of the expectations we have of ourselves and others. When our expectations are unrealistically high, it creates a situation that usually results in stress, anxiety, disappointment and anger. As an example, consider the plight of the type A personality. These are hard-driving individuals who have high expectations for performance from themselves and others. Furthermore, these individuals often react to disappointment with anger and a desire to push through almost any obstacle to achieve their objectives. While some of these people are indeed successful, they are prime candidates for heart disease and often pay a high price for their achievements, including often disrupted or compromised interpersonal relationships.

When individuals have high expectations for performance that include a quest for perfection, the results can be particularly debilitating. Among Latter-day Saints, the Savior's command to "be ye therefore perfect" (Matthew 5:48) is well known and is a goal that that Latter-day Saints aspire to ultimately achieve. The difficulty lies in the belief that perfection needs to happen now—today—and that perfection is a requirement in all aspects of life. If perfection is not achieved, then frustration, low self-worth, and self-deprecation may soon follow.

In addition to the belief that perfection needs to transpire now, there are many who are motivated by menacing internal voices reminding them that their performance is never adequate and if they just tried harder or worked longer they would be able to meet their personal standard of perfection. Unfortunately, unbridled perfectionism can lead to stress, anxiety, depression, and suicidal ideation.

We knew a bishop who keenly felt the weight of his calling and, consequently, set perfectionistic expectations for himself. He believed that it was his responsibility to be at every ward activity and meeting and to always be available to help ward members with their problems. Consequently, he poured much of his time and emotional resources into his calling while neglecting many of his own needs and those of his family members. While he was successful at meeting many of his church responsibilities, he was working at an unsustainable pace and eventually began to experience symptoms of "burnout," resulting from prolonged overstress and a disregard for his personal limits, emotional needs and family relationships.

Perfectionism often masquerades in words such as "should," "must," and "have to," and is associated with "all or none" thinking which may cause us to think that there are only two options: perfection or failure. This leads to expectations such as, "I have to do the presentation perfectly," or "I should never complain," and "I must get the job done exactly right." Even if we are not troubled by a pervasive need to be perfect, many of us succumb to perfectionistic expectations in some areas, such as parenting, job performance, church callings, or school work, and suffer from the persistent pangs of having fallen short.

The Faces of Perfectionism

Underling the need to be perfect is fear, specifically fears of disapproval, criticism, rejection, and failure and associated feelings of shame, guilt and anxiety. The internal dialog of the perfectionist is: "If I am not perfect, I am not worthy"—not worthy of acceptance, love, and being valued by self and others. In addition, flaws, weaknesses, and mistakes are not tolerated; they are viewed as evidence of failure and badness, and there is no room for the idea of being "forgivably human."

Desperately trying to bolster a failing sense of self-esteem, the perfectionist is constantly looking for external validation of worth and value. Accomplishment and productivity may provide some relief, but only if things are done perfectly and without blemish. Unfortunately, this lofty goal is impossible to attain; therefore, no matter how good the performance, the perfectionist is left with the empty feeling of not having achieved enough. Individuals who expect perfection in themselves also have penchant for comparing themselves to others, hoping to see the imperfections in their associates and perhaps to feel some, however slight, sense of superiority. This can lead to an over-emphasis on appearances and impression management.

For example, a Latter-day Saint woman with perfectionistic expectations of herself may try to present an image, to others and herself, of being an organized and stellar homemaker. This woman excels at her part-time job and civic responsibilities and is always nurturing and patient with her children. In addition, she has the perfect Latter-day Saint family complete with a devoted, spiritual husband who is always helpful and never gets mad. Of course, her children are high achieving, obedient, exemplary, and popular. They hold leadership positions at both church and school.

While the woman in the above scenario may experience an illusory sense of validation, it is likely to be fleeting and she will continue to struggle with the same basic issue—she is unable to allow herself to feel acceptable outside of meeting a standard of perfection. When comparing themselves to others, perfectionists are also quick to see their own shortcomings and weaknesses and to view their peers as better or more accomplished. This only intensifies their efforts to hide their missteps and shortcomings, along with feelings of shame and inadequacy, behind a cloak of perfection. The result is a diminished ability to be open and vulnerable, which leads to feeling disconnected and isolated from others.

Those caught in the perfection trap often suffer from overstress and exhaustion because they are always trying to accomplish more, take on another project, make something better or reach another goal.

In and of themselves, accomplishment and goal attainment are not bad things, but for the perfectionist, there is little pleasure in doing them. Instead, there is a compulsive drive to meet the demands of an internal critic that will accept nothing less than the best. Consequently, it is difficult to find a sense of contentment and satisfaction because there is always one more thing to do, one more goal to achieve, and the endless grind of never feeling good enough.

Unhealthy Efforts to Cope with Perfectionism

In the midst of this battle, it is not unusual for people to turn to unhealthy sources of relief from the relentless emotional onslaught that comes from always falling short. Some may begin to self-medicate, turning to substances such as alcohol, prescription medications, and illegal drugs. Others crave food, indulge in pornography, or engage in compulsive sexual behavior. Retreating to the virtual reality of internet relationships, persistent gaming, and long hours of watching television are also common.

Ted had a client who seemed to have the ideal life. She was a successful professional and had a wonderful husband and beautiful children. She had the means to travel the world and enjoyed many luxuries and pleasures. She held important and visible callings in the Church, was active in civic affairs, and was admired by friends, family, and associates alike. Unfortunately, she was unhappy and overstressed. This woman felt as though she was constantly falling short, not doing all she should and unable to live up to the standards and expectations that others had for her. Consequently, she was plagued by unrelenting feelings of guilt, frustration, and shame that led to self-contempt and occasional suicidal feelings.

In an effort to gain some relief from her internal pain, she began abusing prescription medications. Initially, the medicine seemed helpful, and she was able to regulate her use to some degree. However, it soon became a gripping addiction, which, over time, profoundly impacted all aspects of her life. By the time her closest associates intervened to help, her addiction had disrupted her relationship with her husband and children, undermined her competency at work and church, and eroded her physical and mental health to the point that she needed to be hospitalized and then transferred to a substance abuse treatment center.

Fortunately, this woman was blessed with people around her who were willing to take the necessary steps to direct her to the help she needed. After several months of treatment, she was able to not only overcome the addiction but also gain an understanding of the psychological and spiritual factors that contributed to the problem. Specifically, she began to see the role that her own perfectionism and unrealistic expectations played in her stress and unhappiness, particularly as it involved her feelings of never doing enough, or being enough, and a constant sense of being less than she should be. The client also gained a new understanding and appreciation of the Atonement of Jesus Christ and of the Savior's offer to love, empower, and redeem us in spite of our flaws and imperfections.

Healthier Perspectives

Modifying our tendencies toward perfectionism and overly high expectations is an important part of managing our lives; in fact, this may require some rethinking of the role of perfection in the gospel plan. While our goal is to become like our Heavenly Father and His Son, Jesus Christ, and to become perfect as they are, it is important to remember that perfection is a process and will, ultimately, not be achieved until the next life.

Perfection can only be attained gradually "line upon line, precept upon precept," and only as a result of our own efforts in company with the grace of our Savior. In his final exhortations, Moroni counseled us, "Yea, come unto Christ, and be perfected in him . . . and if ye . . . love God with all your might, mind and strength, then is his grace sufficient for you, that by his grace ye may be perfect in Christ."[2] A modern Prophet, President Russell M. Nelson has encouragingly stated, "Meanwhile, brothers and sisters, let us do the best we can and try to improve each day. When our imperfections appear, we can keep trying to correct them. . . . We need not be dismayed if our earnest efforts toward perfection now seem so arduous and endless. Perfection is pending. It can come in full only after the Resurrection and only through the Lord."[3]

Our goal, therefore, is incremental improvement, trying to "stay in the game" and progress, line upon line. Ultimately we rely upon Jesus Christ, through the enabling power of His Atonement, to augment our efforts to become better and eventually attain perfection and eternal life.

In describing this process, Elder Bruce R. McConkie of the Quorum of the Twelve Apostles declared, "As members of the Church, if we chart a course leading to eternal life; if we begin the processes of spiritual rebirth, and are going in the right direction; if we chart a course of sanctifying our souls, and degree by degree are going in that direction; . . . then it is absolutely guaranteed—there is no question whatever about it—we shall gain eternal life."[4]

Elder Devin Cornish of the Seventy elaborated on this topic in his talk in the October 2016 General Conference:

> Let me be direct and clear. The answers to the questions "Am I good enough?" and "Will I make it?" are "Yes! You are going to be good enough" and "Yes, you are going to make it as long as you keep repenting and do not rationalize or rebel." The God of heaven is not a heartless referee looking for any excuse to throw us out of the game. He is our perfectly loving Father, who yearns more than anything else to have all of His children come back home and live with Him as families forever. . . . Our Heavenly Father intends for us to make it! That is His work and His glory.
>
> I love the way President Gordon B. Hinckley used to teach this principle. I heard him say on several occasions, "Brothers and sisters, all the Lord expects of us is to try, but you have to really try!"
>
> "Really trying" means doing the best we can, recognizing where we need to improve, and then trying again. By repeatedly doing this, we come closer and closer to the Lord, we feel His Spirit more and more, and we receive more of His grace, or help.[5]

If the desires of our hearts are to love and serve God, and if we strive to repent, serve others, obey the commandments, and develop

Christlike attributes, He will enable us to achieve what we are striving for, both in this life and in the next.

Our efforts to improve require patience with ourselves as we struggle with weaknesses, mistakes and imperfections. Patterns of thinking, feeling and behaving typically change slowly and only with consistent effort. Criticizing and demeaning ourselves is not only unfair, but significantly hinders our efforts to improve. Each of us should view ourselves as a "work in progress" and incorporate an attitude of acceptance alongside our desires to change. Commenting on this concept, Elder Jeffrey R. Holland said, "Our only hope for true perfection is in receiving it as a gift from heaven—we can't 'earn' it. Thus, the grace of Christ offers us not only salvation from sorrow and sin and death but also salvation from our own persistent self-criticism.[6]

It is also helpful to keep in mind the actual meaning of perfection. The term denotes a state of completeness or wholeness as opposed to being without flaw or defect.[7] From this perspective, our goal is to engage in a process of self-improvement and to develop ourselves, as opposed to focusing primarily on eliminating mistakes, faults and imperfections. Elder Dallin Oaks has stated, "The gospel of Jesus Christ is a plan that shows us how to become what our Heavenly Father desires us to become . . . the Final Judgment is not just an evaluation of the sum total of good and evil acts—what we have done. It is an acknowledgment of the final effect of our acts and thoughts— what we have become."[8]

It is helpful to view our efforts to change as a developmental process where we incrementally improve over time, as we strive to become more like our Savior. This endeavor creates hope, energy and positive motivation. Furthermore, we must remember that we do not have to make all of these improvements overnight, nor by ourselves. It is notable in this regard that Joseph Smith once stated, "I never told you I was perfect, but there is no error in the revelations I have taught."[9] As exemplified by the Prophet, even in our imperfect and flawed state, we can move forward and, with the Lord's help, become better and accomplish many good things in our lives.

Dealing with Perfectionism

If you struggle with perfectionism, as many of us do, there are some specific strategies that could also be helpful to incorporate into your daily efforts to combat this problem.

1. Perfection is not required to succeed. The first thing to consider is that perfection is not required to succeed; hence, you do not have to be flawless in your performance to be successful. The most accomplished individuals in any given area have achieved their status by walking a path that usually includes many mistakes, false starts, unimpressive efforts and failures. For example, President Abraham Lincoln ran for office and was defeated six times before he was ever nominated for President. In fact, it is often through our lackluster performances, faulty decisions, and poor efforts that we improve and grow. The key is that we are trying, that we do not get discouraged because of our mistakes, and that we do not give up. Remember what President Russell M. Nelson taught: "the Lord loves effort, because effort brings rewards that can't come without it."[10]

2. Excellence instead of perfection. Adopting a goal of excellence instead of perfection can also be useful. Excellence denotes reaching a high level of competence or merit but does not include being perfect. Excellence also allows room for mistakes, falling short in some areas at some times, and not doing everything right. For example, former BYU and NFL Hall of Fame quarterback Steve Young is one of the all-time NFL leaders in pass completion percentage, completing 64.3 percent of his passes. While this is an impressive statistic, it is also true that more than a third of his passes were incomplete, a performance that was a far cry from perfection. Likewise, a professional quarterback might play an excellent game but still have incomplete passes, overthrow open receivers, and take a sack or two. Excelling is the act of achieving challenging, but attainable goals. Such a quest is stimulating and exciting. All too often, if individuals are seeking for perfection and do not attain it, they feel demoralized.

3. Dare to be average. In his book, Feeling Good, Dr. David Burns proposes the idea that those who struggle with perfectionism should

"Dare to be Average."[11] In a somewhat paradoxical approach, he suggests that those who struggle with perfectionism would do well by striving to be average. This will not be an easy task since many perfectionists believe that if they give up their perfectionistic strivings they will not perform effectively or achieve their goals. Further, they may be in danger of letting people down or opening themselves up for criticism.

In any case, he recommends engaging in an experiment where standards of performance are reduced and then outcomes and satisfaction with the task are evaluated. Specifically, he suggests choosing an activity, and instead of striving for 100 percent performance, individuals should aim for 80 percent, then 60 percent and finally 40 percent performance. Afterwards, individuals should evaluate how well they performed and how much they enjoyed the task. He predicted that both performance and satisfaction levels would go up.

Since I (Ted) have some perfectionistic tendencies, I was intrigued with Dr. Burns's thinking and decided to put his experiment to the test while working on this chapter. After getting my head around the idea of reducing my performance expectations, which took some doing, I found that when I eased up on myself and reduced my expectations, the writing became easier, I enjoyed the process more, and the quality did not suffer. I'm not sure the quality improved, but the experience was more enjoyable, and I was probably more creative. You might try this experiment with some task that brings out your perfectionistic tendencies such as writing a talk, giving a presentation, studying for a test, or parenting your children and see if it works for you.

4. Time limits on tasks. Another strategy worth trying is placing a time limit on all tasks that you do for a week. Those who need to do things perfectly usually procrastinate and put off tasks, and when they finally get around to doing it, they take a longer time because they want to get it "right," avoid mistakes, and turn out a perfect product. Limiting the time in which you can accomplish something forces you to do it imperfectly because you do not have enough time to get everything right. You just have to complete it, move on, and have the experience of trying to be all right with a less than optimal, less than perfect result. For most tasks, this process works fine. In fact it is likely that the task will be less stressful and the process more enjoyable, or at least less annoying.

5. Accept the law of averages. For those of us who are proficient at consistently expecting excellent performances from ourselves in whatever we are engaged in at any given time, it is important to remember that statistically speaking, it is not possible for us to perform above our personal average all the time. Sometimes we are going to do exceptionally well, and other times our performance will be mediocre in comparison to how well we usually do.

To use another example from the world of sports, a major league baseball player who is a great hitter will probably have a batting average around .300. This means that, on average, he will get a hit approximately three out of every ten times at bat. It is not uncommon for a hitter of this caliber to get a hit 3 out of 5 times at bat in a particular game for an average of .600 for that game, and in a subsequent game, get 0 hits in 5 at bats for an average of .000. Experienced baseball players usually do not get too upset about this because they understand the ebb and flow of hitting and realize that if they do not hit well in one game, they are likely to do better in the next.

As an example from my own life, I (Ted) have a church calling where I am often asked to speak in worship and training meetings. During the first few months of my calling, I realized, much to my dismay, that I was not able to give a stellar message every time I spoke to a church group. Sometimes the thoughts and words flowed well, and I thought I did a pretty good job. On other occasions, I seemed to have trouble putting my thoughts together and articulating them as I intended. When this happened, I often criticized myself for not doing a better job—not preparing well, not focusing enough, not speaking with the spirit, etc. Finally, I realized that no matter how hard I tried, some talks were going to be better than others, and my best course was to accept that reality and adjust my expectations accordingly. While I am still disappointed in myself at times, I have been much less stressed about my performance, and my calling has been more enjoyable.

Realizing that our performance on the tasks and demands we face daily are (hopefully) generally acceptable but are likely to vary from great to average to not worth mentioning, depending on the day, can help us maintain a realistic perspective about our expectations and save us a good deal of stress, self-criticism, and unproductive worry.

6. *Change your perfectionistic language.* Another strategy is to monitor the kind of language you use when you think about your expectations for performance or evaluate how you have done. For example, if you find yourself using phrases such as "I should . . ." or "I must . . ." or "I have to," you are likely making demands of yourself that are unrealistic and making judgments of performance that are rigid and inflexible. For example, if you tell yourself, "I should stay calm in every situation" or "I must do a great job on my presentation" or "I have to look my best at all times," you are probably going to fail and end up stressed and dissatisfied with yourself.

The alternative to this way of thinking is to realize that those things you feel that you should, must, or have to do are just aspirations or preferences that might happen but may not and are really not as necessary to your well-being and happiness as you might think. For example, instead of saying, "I should stay calm in every situation," it would be a healthier to say "I would like to be calm in every situation, and I will try, but it might not happen." Consider another example. Instead of saying, "I have to look my best when I go to church," you could say, "I would prefer to look my best when I go to church, but some days it is not going to happen." By cultivating a more flexible and reasonable way of looking at what you want or need and realizing that these wants are not essential—but simply desirable and preferable—you can sidestep a significant amount of anxiety and stress.

7. *Identify and challenge your underlying fears.* As mentioned above, perfectionism is essentially caused by fear. Fear of what? While it may vary somewhat among individuals, most perfectionists are afraid that if they are not perfect, they will incur criticism, displeasure, and disapproval from those around them. Even if the individuals they associate with in their lives are not critical or judgmental, it is the internalized critic that they are afraid to displease. The voice inside our heads that is telling us we have to "get it right" or "do it with no mistakes." This voice is often that of a critical parental figure that may represent an actual parent or other critical adult from the past.

Beyond fears of criticism and judgment, perfectionism at the core is a way to stave off fears of rejection and loss of love. The perfectionist fears that if things are not done perfectly, then they will ultimately be shunned or rejected and lose the love of the people they need most. Another way of looking at it is that perfectionists at some level believe that to gain acceptance and love from others, they must prove their worth by doing everything right. This often takes the form of the perfectionist continuing to believe that if they could only do things perfectly, without flaw, then they would earn the love and acceptance they most deeply desire.

If the underlying fears associated with perfectionistic thinking can be identified, then steps can be taken to challenge and replace them with more realistic perspectives. One way to identify these fears is to ask yourself questions, such as

- "What am I afraid will happen if I fall short of my expectations?"
- "Who will I displease?"
- "What will people think of me if I fall short?"
- "What will I think of myself if I do not perform admirably?"

Once you have answered these questions, you can begin to challenge the validity of your fears and reconsider your effort to do things perfectly. For example, you could ask yourself, "Will people really criticize me if I do not perform admirably or if I make a mistake?" Even better is to assess how people actually do react when you think you have not performed well. Are they actually critical, shaming or rejecting? In many cases the answer is probably not, or at least not to the degree that you expect. In addition, the question can also be asked, "So what if people are not pleased with my effort or level achievement?" "How bad is that?," "Will it really affect me that much?" Once again, probably not as much as expected.

A man entered therapy at his wife's urging because he was irritable and easily frustrated at home and would frequently "blow up" over little things. He was a successful attorney who felt that his work had to be flawless, with no room for error. He also had real trouble taking time off for vacations; he felt he always needed to be available for his clients so he could do best the best possible job for them.

Through the course of working with his therapist, he revealed that he had been raised by a scrutinizing and critical mother who expected correct behavior and flawless performance in school and other activities. This man adopted her perfectionistic attitudes and had spent most of his life trying to please the critical mother that he carried around in his mind. He feared that anything less than perfect performance would result in embarrassment and humiliation and, at a deeper level, the loss of love and approval from people around him.

Once he understood this and realized where these fears originated, he was prepared to challenge their validity and modify them. For example, he asked his wife how she would feel if he did not always stay on top of the family finances or made mistakes with the budget. He also asked co-workers how they viewed their own mistakes, which helped him realize that most of them were much less fearful about making mistakes than he was. This gave him some confidence to try new ways of thinking about his performance and what would realistically happen if he fell short, made mistakes, and did not always do things right. Over time, he became less tense and calmer. Consequently, the blow-ups and irritability at home decreased significantly.

8. Be open about imperfections. It can also be therapeutic to identify your imperfections and then try to be more accepting and open with others about them. It is interesting that people who consistently present themselves as "having it all together" may inadvertently push people away because they seem unapproachable. On the other hand, those who are more willing to admit and embrace their weaknesses and mistakes come across as more open, authentic, and vulnerable. This, in turn, often makes them more attractive to others and it is easier for them to form meaningful interpersonal connections. We are aware of a particular set of parents who decided that their family was perfect. They often told other parents that they had no problems with their children. Although these "perfect" parents felt this approach was a way to elevate their status in their ward and stake, it actually drove people away. No one seemed to be able to relate to a "perfect family."

9. Being "good enough." Finally, a helpful approach for those struggling with perfectionism is the concept of being *good enough*. In the

1950s, pediatrician and psychoanalyst Donald Winnicott coined the term "good enough mother."[12] With this phrase, Winnicott was referring to the idea that there are no perfect mothers—mothers who are perfectly sensitive and attuned to the needs of their children, and whose responses are always in sync with what their child needs at any given moment. However, there are "good enough" mothers who understand their children's needs and feelings most of the time and usually, but not always, respond to their children in ways that are helpful, thus enabling their healthy development.

By the same token, there are good enough fathers, good enough children, good enough spouses, good enough friends, and good enough disciples of Christ—none of them perfect but good enough to achieve important goals; have meaningful, loving relationships; live fulfilling, happy lives; feel a sense of peace and contentment; and qualify for the saving grace of Jesus Christ. President Brigham Young taught, "We all occupy diversified stations in the world, and in the Kingdom of God. Those who do right, and seek the glory of the Father in Heaven, whether their knowledge be little or much, or whether they can do little or much, if they do the very best they know how, they are perfect."[13] All we need to do is the best that we can. That is all that our Father in Heaven expects from us.

As we strive daily to keep an accurate perspective of the role of perfection in the plan of salvation and manage our expectations accordingly we are free to focus on trying to make small, incremental changes in ourselves which will gradually result in our developing a more Christlike character. The process of seeing ourselves change, coupled with the magnificent power of the Atonement of Jesus Christ, instills in us feelings of peace, hope, and well-being.

References to Chapter 5

1   Glennon Doyle Melton, *Love Warrior*, (New York: Flatiron, 2017).

2   Moroni 10:32

3   Russell M. Nelson, "Perfection Pending," *Ensign*, November 1995.

4   Bruce R. McConkie, "Jesus Christ and Him Crucified," BYU Speeches, September 5, 1976.

5   J. Devn Cornish, "Am I Good Enough? Will I Make It?," *Ensign*, November 2016.

6   Jeffrey R. Holland, "Be Ye Therefore Perfect," *Ensign*, November 2017.

7   Russell M. Nelson, "Perfection Pending," *Ensign*, November 1995.

8   Dallin H. Oaks, "The Challenge to Become," *Ensign*, November 2000.

9   *Teachings of the Prophet Joseph Smith*, sel. Joseph Fielding Smith (1976), 368.

10 Russell M. Nelson, as cited in Joy D. Jones, "An Especially Noble Calling," *Ensign*, May 2020.

11 David D. Burns, *Feeling Good: The New Mood Therapy* (William Morrow: New York, 1980).

12 See Donald D. Winnicott, *Playing and Reality* (Routledge: London, 1971).

13 Brigham Young, "Discourse," *Deseret News*, 31 August 1854, 1; cited by LeGrand R. Curtis, *Ensign*, July 1995, 34.

Chapter 6

CULTIVATING MEANINGFUL RELATIONSHIPS

Let us resolve to cherish those we love by spending meaningful time with them, doing things together, and cultivating treasured memories.

—President Dieter F. Uchtdorf [1]

DEVELOPING AND MAINTAINING meaningful relationships with others is a basic human desire and a key to finding happiness and peace in life. Most humans share a need for connection and affiliation. In fact, much of our time and energy is spent on trying to initiate, improve, or repair our relationships. The theology of The Church of Jesus Christ of Latter-Day Saints emphasizes the importance of family relationships in the plan of happiness and as an essential pre-requisite for exaltation.[2] In "The Family: A Proclamation to the World," the First Presidency and Quorum of the Twelve Apostles declared,

> We, the First Presidency and the Council of the Twelve Apostles of The Church of Jesus Christ of Latter-day Saints, solemnly proclaim that marriage between a man and a woman is ordained of God and that the family is central to the Creator's plan for the eternal destiny of His children. . . . The divine plan of happiness enables family relationships to be perpetuated beyond the grave. Sacred ordinances and covenants available in holy temples make it possible for

individuals to return to the presence of God and for families to be united eternally.[3]

Meaningful friendships are also viewed as desirable and an important part of our mortal and post-mortal experience. Joseph Smith taught that "friendship is one of the grand keys of Mormonism,"[4] and in a revelation in 1833, the Lord revealed to the Prophet, "And that same sociality which exists among us here will exist among us there, only it will be coupled with eternal glory, which glory we do not now enjoy."[5]

Research in human development indicates that we are "hardwired" for relationships and that our early attachments to caregivers form the foundation and the context for our psychological development.[6] Establishing a secure base in childhood lays the groundwork for the healthy development of self-esteem, emotional control, initiative, and sociality. It is also clear that secure connections with others are essential for optimal emotional development and a sense of well-being throughout our lives. Moreover, our spiritual progression is strongly impacted by the nature of our relationships with parents, spouses, children, teachers, mentors and, ultimately, with the Savior.

Scientific studies have also revealed that people who have close relationships are happier and healthier than those who do not. Among other things, those who have strong ties to family and friends are less stressed and depressed and are less likely to have a stroke, heart disease, or experience early cognitive decline.[7] In fact, a longitudinal study conducted by researchers at Harvard followed hundreds of people for seventy-five years. They identified the quality of people's relationships as the single clearest predictor of their physical health, longevity and quality of life.[8]

On the other hand, a lack of meaningful relationships is associated with higher levels of stress, anxiety, depression, and a shorter lifespan. In one study, social isolation was as impactful on mortality as smoking and alcohol consumption and was more detrimental to individual health than obesity or not exercising. This study, conducted at Brigham Young University, indicated further that the influence of poor social relationships on the risk of death was equivalent to smoking up to fifteen cigarettes a day.[9]

The emotional impact of social isolation was clearly demonstrated during the recent Covid-19 pandemic. Data from the U.S. Census Bureau in April and May of 2020, a period of time where strict social distancing measures were in force in most parts of our nation, indicated that the national rate of anxiety and depression tripled compared to the same months in 2019. While this increase was likely a result of several factors, social isolation and loneliness were among the most salient.[10]

More generally, one survey revealed that two-thirds of Americans often or always feel lonely,[11] while another study found a three-fold increase over the past two decades in the number of people who have no confidants.[12] Factors contributing to this trend include living fast-paced and transitory lifestyles, dual career families, and social media, which reinforces less person-to-person interaction, and a culture that is increasingly focused on appearance and superficiality.

In addition to societal factors, there are individualized reasons that people struggle with developing meaningful relationships. A few months ago, Ted sent an informal survey to a group of Facebook friends asking them: 1) Do you feel you have meaningful relationships in your life? And 2) what gets in the way of having those kinds of relationships? About 20 people responded to the survey, with 60 percent indicating that they had several meaningful relationships and 40 percent reporting that they had few or none. In regard to what interferes with relationships, the most common response was that individuals were too busy and had little time. Other reasons included a lack of interest, feeling that it would be too much work, difficulty trusting others, and fears of rejection and disappointment.

Since we have already established the importance of positive interpersonal relationships for physical and mental health, as well as spiritual well-being, ask yourself the following questions:

How am I doing in my relationships?

Would I like to have more meaningful and satisfying relationships with family members and friends?

What can I do to improve the quality of my relationships?

What sacrifices am I willing to make in order to develop deeper relationships with those around me?

Here are some suggestions for establishing strong relationships with others.

1. Reach Out

If you are in the position of wanting to develop new relationships or improve the quality of existing ones, the first step is to take responsibility for making changes and intentionally reach out to others. Do not wait for others to come to you! Take the initiative! Whether you are looking for a romantic relationship or a friend, you will need to face the reality that developing new relationships is challenging for most people, especially as we get older, and you will have to push through inertia and perhaps anxiety to get started. Mark shares the following experience:

> Years ago, we moved to McKinney, Texas, a suburb of Dallas. At that time, the area was growing rapidly. The week that we moved into our new ward, so did six other families—and that's how it seemed to go about every weekend for several months. It was difficult to detect who was new in the ward, and who had been there for a while. Consequently, many new families lay back and waited for others to reach out to them. We decided to take a different approach. Instead of waiting for people to come to us—we came to them. We invited people to our home for Sunday dinners and get-togethers. Within a short amount of time, we felt connected to the ward, and our children had many friends. Taking the initiative can make all the difference in building relationships. We are here to act, and not be acted upon.

Moreover, it could be most helpful to put yourself in places where you can meet and get to know people. Joining groups, organizations, and clubs where there are people in your age range and who have interests similar to yours is a good start. These groups might focus on things such as volunteer work, hobbies, church activities, athletic interests, or learning new skills. For example, you could join a gym or cycling club, take a class, become part of a craft guild or volunteer with the Red Cross. Even organizing a block party in your neighborhood could glean tremendous benefits.

Furthermore, reaching out to people who you already have some familiarity with but have not formally met, such as neighbors, co-workers, or church members is also an option. During the many months that the coronavirus pandemic kept most people at home and more secluded, Ted and his wife, Laura, began taking frequent walks in their neighborhood where they often ran into neighbors that they may have seen before but never met. Ted relates,

It was an enjoyable experience to stop, introduce ourselves, and have a brief conversation with these individuals. Our talks usually focused on such things as how long they had lived in the neighborhood, what their children and other family members were doing, and their reactions to quarantine and the pandemic generally. We made it a point to memorize the names of those we met so we could refer to them by name at subsequent street meetings. We became acquainted with many interesting and friendly people on our walks, and are hopeful that some of these acquaintances will turn into more involved friendships over time.

For relationships that already exist, you may need to initiate a conversation or extend an invitation to reconnect. Reaching out to a family member or friend with whom you would like to become closer, or have not seen or talked to in some time, can spark new interest and involvement. During the coronavirus pandemic, we knew several people who started reaching out to old friends they had not been in contact with for some time. Some of these relationships had just gradually faded over time and while others had changed because of moves or changes in lifestyle. The response to their efforts was surprisingly positive and gratifying. Their conversations with these old friends included catching up on the happenings in their lives, reminiscing about past experiences together, and talking about interests and future plans. In each case, the relationships were rekindled, at least to some degree, and a door was opened to ongoing communication and continuing the relationship.

Something we have learned from these experiences is that most people respond well when you reach out to them in a non-threatening way, with an attitude of friendship and a genuine desire to establish a connection. Most people seem to welcome the opportunity to share their thoughts and ideas and are especially appreciative when you listen with interest to what they are communicating. As you gradually become more familiar with one another, and it is your desire for the friendship to progress, you might extend an invitation to do something outside the environment where you normally interact, such as going to lunch or dinner or attending a community event. If all goes well, then it is mostly a matter of scheduling times to get together and work on deepening the relationship.

2. Prioritize Relationships

Oftentimes our need is not necessarily to make new connections with people, but to improve the relationships you already have. Whether it involves a spouse, parent, other family member, or a friendship, moving this relationship toward the top of your priority ladder is essential. Carving out time to have meaningful interactions with others, especially those closest to us, can be difficult in the busy, faced-paced world in which we live. This challenge is intensified by the temptation to communicate primarily through the internet, particularly social media. Commenting on this, Elder Dieter F. Uchtdorf stated,

> In our day it is easy to merely pretend to spend time with others. With the click of a mouse, we can "connect" with thousands of "friends" without ever having to face a single one of them. Technology can be a wonderful thing, and it is useful when we cannot be near our loved ones. My wife and I live far away from precious family members; we know how that is. However, I believe that we are not headed in the right direction, individually and as a society, when we connect with family or friends mostly by reposting humorous pictures,

forwarding trivial things, or linking our loved ones to sites on the Internet. I suppose there is a place for this kind of activity, but how much time are we willing to spend on it? If we fail to give our best personal self and undivided time to those who are truly important to us, one day we will regret it.

Let us resolve to cherish those we love by spending meaningful time with them, doing things together, and cultivating treasured memories.[13]

One way to spend meaningful time together is to establish ritualized interactions. For a married couple, this might be having a regular time at the end of each day for conversation and reconnecting. With a friend it could be a regular lunch date or a daily appointment for a walk or workout at the gym. The important thing is that the experience is pleasant and enjoyable, and that there is an opportunity for meaningful communication.

Furthermore, it is important for each person in a relationship to initiate and respond positively to bids from the other for connection and closeness. The desire to connect is universal and engenders feelings of security and well-being. This is especially true at times when a person feels insecure or unsure, and might be struggling with any number of concerns, such as fears of rejection, or worries about feeling incompetent, unworthy, or unimportant. For a couple, the bid for connection might be an invitation from the partner to hold hands, hug, or express love or appreciation verbally. In a friendship, the invitation for connection might be a request to talk about a problem or concern or an invitation to attend an upcoming event together.

While face-to-face communication is fundamental to meaningful relationships, consistent and reciprocal communication that occurs between in-person interactions, such as phone calls, texts and messages on social media, also serve to deepen interpersonal bonds. In addition, expressing appreciation and love to others, and letting them know that you value your relationship with them, promotes connectedness and positivity along with an enhanced sense of well-being for all involved.

3. Become a Listener

For any relationship to be fulfilling there must be effective communication. But what exactly does that mean? The first and most important communication skill, and perhaps the most difficult, is listening. It sounds easy, but listening attentively and empathically is hard work. To do it, you first need to be willing to take time out from whatever you are doing or thinking about and open your mind to the expressions of the other person. This will take focus, which will require you to turn your attention to the expressions and comments of the other person with the sole purpose to gain understanding—that is—to see things the way they see them. A good listener will suspend their own reactions and desires to speak. When you listen to someone attentively, you are communicating to him or her that that you care about them and that what they say is important. Being truly heard is a validating experience, and hearing and understanding is one of the highest expressions of love and respect.

The best word to describe this kind of listening is "presence," which means being fully focused, interested in, and open to the words and feelings being communicated without interrupting. You probably only really know what "presence" means if you have had the experience of being in a conversation with another person who is fully focused on what you are saying and is genuinely interested in understanding what you are trying to communicate.

Ted relates the following experience:

When I was a student in college, I had a conversation with one of my professors, who was also an accomplished psychotherapist. I had been struggling with several anxieties and frustrations that I had difficulty fully understanding and communicating. From the first moments of our conversation, I could sense that this was not your normal professor-student interaction. He was very much present and I could sense his undistracted focus and genuine interest in understanding what I was trying to communicate. It was one of the few times I had felt fully understood by someone who was invested in genuinely and attentively listening to me. Once I felt understood, the solutions to my struggles became more manageable and within grasp.

Effective communication is also reciprocal in nature and includes mutual validation of experience. One person does not dominate the conversation, but there is space for each person to express their views, ideas, and feelings. Each person is attentive to the other and genuinely interested in what is being said. Asking questions is a wonderful way to show that we are listening and that we care about them. Furthermore, validating communication contains expressions of understanding, empathy, and support and is empowering and healing.

For example, if a friend or family member is struggling with the stresses of parenting and work, one response might be, "I can understand why you feel this way, you have a lot on your plate right now and it sometimes gets overwhelming." Validating responses often contain words of affirmation. For a person who is experiencing a recent setback you could say, "It is pretty hard when you really want to accomplish something and it doesn't work out. I want you to know that I have confidence in you and your ability to bounce back and succeed."

4. Share Vulnerabilities

Much of our communication with others is focused on routine, mundane and superficial matters in life. In marital relationships, superficial communication often takes the form of coordination. Consider the following examples:

- "What time is the appointment?"
- "Which after school activities do the kids have today?"
- "I want to eat dinner at this restaurant."

To be sure, these are necessary communications, but they are all relatively superficial. For relationships to become closer and more meaningful, there has to be a willingness on both sides to share on a deeper, more personal level. Such disclosures include sharing hopes, dreams, aspirations and goals. It may also include talking about vulnerabilities, fears, weaknesses, and feelings of inadequacy.

One way to know that you are communicating in this level is when you experience a sense of vulnerability during the interaction. More specifically, you are aware of the possibility that the response from the person you are talking with could cause you to feel embarrassed, ashamed, hurt, demeaned, or rejected. For example, a man might disclose to his wife, "I sometimes worry that I am not good enough for you. You have such wonderful qualities and talents, and I feel that I am lacking in comparison." This disclosure would certainly require this man to have courage and trust in his wife because her response could be hurtful if it was negative or dismissive. On the other hand, if she responded with understanding and some open disclosure on her part, it could open a dialogue that would allow further openness and the sharing of mutual vulnerabilities. In this scenario, his wife might respond, "I had no idea you felt that way. It is surprising to me because I look at you as the confident one who has it all together, while I often feel very unsure of myself."

Some people prefer to avoid self-disclosure, preferring instead to "play it safe." While they might side-step embarrassment or rejection, they also lose the opportunity to develop deep, intimate bonds that are sustaining and healing. It is natural to avoid self-disclosing if you feel a lack of trust with another person. However, it takes some degree of self-disclosure to actually build the foundation of trust that is required to be able to disclose more intimate thoughts and feelings.

5. Understand the Healing Power of Relationships

Relationships where there exists an emotionally meaningful connection can be both transforming and healing. It is probably safe to say that each of us has experienced some type of disappointment, injury, or rejection in our past relationships with parents, siblings, friends, romantic partners, and spouses. Interestingly, the effects of these experiences usually raise their heads in some form in current relationships, especially with spouses and close friends.

As an example, a man who was emotionally neglected by his parents in childhood may develop a sensitivity to what he believes to be neglectful behavior by his spouse. In response, he withdraws from her and occasionally becomes angry and accusatory. If he and his wife are unable to communicate in a way that facilitates understanding and working through the issue, the problem will likely continue and may, in essence, become a repeat performance of what happened in his childhood with his parents.

On the other hand, if this couple share a desire to face the problem together, and have the ability to communicate in an honest, respectful, and validating way, then the husband would have the opportunity to talk openly about feeling neglected by his wife, and she could express her reactions and views about it. Their conversation would, hopefully, progress to a discussion about what he might do to address his issue of sensitivity to feeling neglected and what she can do to help him feel more caring from her. This type of interaction has a high probability to be healing for him and strengthening to their marital relationship.

As demonstrated in this example, injuries experienced in earlier relationships tend to influence how a person behaves and reacts in current relationships. This can lead to misunderstandings, overreactions and conflict. If these difficulties are addressed in a relationship where there is trust and understanding, relationship struggles can often be worked out, and there can also be healing from past relationship injuries.

6. Resolve Conflict

At some point in every close relationship, there will be differences of opinion and disagreements that can lead to conflict. While conflict is usually uncomfortable and can cause problems in a relationship, if handled correctly, it can usually be resolved and, ultimately, can result in greater closeness and understanding.

Successful resolution of conflict begins with each person's effort to maintain control of his or her emotions. Most of the damage that is done during a disagreement occurs when emotions, especially anger, have escalated to the point where good judgment and concern for the feelings of the other person are compromised. Removing yourself from the situation, calling a "time out," or stopping for a few deep breaths may be necessary to de-escalate and stop the angry expressions.

Once emotional control has been re-established, there can be productive dialogue that focuses on understanding what happened and why. Establishing ground rules during these conversations, such as refraining from name calling, accusing, attacking and blaming can be helpful. A charitable attitude and a genuine interest in understanding the other person's viewpoint and the reasons for their reactions goes a long way toward resolving the problem. Of equal importance is a willingness to recognize and take responsibility for one's contribution to the problem, along with offering apologies and asking for (and giving) forgiveness.

7. Repair Ruptures

In addition to conflict, ruptures in relationships can occur for other reasons, including little time spent together, a lack of interest in nurturing the relationship, distancing by one or both parties, and preoccupations with work, hobbies or other relationships. In each case, if there is a willingness by each party to acknowledge and communicate about the rupture, and to engage in reparative efforts, then solutions can be reached.

An example of a relationship rupture is a couple struggling over how much time the husband spends away from home. Specifically, his wife believes that her husband is spending too much time with work and church responsibilities and puts their relationship as a low priority. On the other hand, he believes that his wife does not understand that he is just trying to fulfill his obligations to provide and serve in the church. She feels frustrated and hurt, and he feels misunderstood and defensive. In this case, if both people are willing to engage in reparative efforts, such as mutual listening, understanding, negotiation, compromise, and problem solving, they will have a good chance of transforming the rupture into a growth experience where their relationship is not only repaired, but ultimately becomes stronger.

Sometimes relationship ruptures occur because of jealousy, competitiveness or envy. We can categorize these feelings as elements of pride, which President Ezra Taft Benson called "the universal sin."[14] The temptation to elevate oneself by putting down or devaluing another is universal and is manifested in a number of ways, including a focus on self, lack of interest in the needs and feelings of others, criticism, boasting or bragging (however subtle), unwillingness to offer praise or acknowledge the achievements of the other person , and withholding love and support.

To keep pride, in all its faces, from undermining important relationships, requires daily attention and effort. The most valuable armament in this battle is humility, which involves an acknowledgment of our own flaws and weaknesses, our propensity to make mistakes and to fall short, and an acceptance of the weaknesses and imperfections of others.

Humility can be cultivated by understanding our dependence on God and others and realizing that lifting others does not diminish ourselves. It is enhanced by expressing gratitude and appreciation, apologizing and forgiving, offering compliments and praise, and moving past comparisons and competition. The humble person "has a broken heart and contrite spirit" and is genuinely happy for the successes, progress, and goodness of others and finds satisfaction in helping those around them to become better.

Speaking on this subject as it applies to marital relationships, Sister Linda K. Burton, former General Relief Society President, has taught, "In a chapter about families, the Church handbook contains this statement: 'The nature of male and female spirits is such that they complete each other.' Please note that it does not say 'compete with each other' but 'complete each other'! We are here to help, lift, and rejoice with each other as we try to become our very best selves . . . When we seek to 'complete' rather than 'compete,' it is so much easier to cheer each other on!"[15]

8. Your Relationship with God

Among all the relationships with which you are involved, the most important is your relationship with our Heavenly Father. Just as you can nurture and cultivate your relationships with other mortals here on the earth, you can likewise nurture your relationship with God.

The most important tool in nurturing this relationship is your communications with Him through prayer. As with relationships here, your communicating with your Heavenly Father can be infrequent, devoid of real meaning, and hampered by a lack of trust in Him. On the other hand, if you believe that He is there, that He truly loves and cares for you, and that His only desire is to bless and help you, then you are in a position to pray with faith and with real intent.

Consequently, you can then open up to him with all of your concerns, aspirations, and needs.

When you open your heart to your Heavenly Father, He will respond and reveal His feelings toward you, which will help you to develop a stronger connection to Him. This connection will help and sustain you through all of your challenges, fears, and trials and will give you a greater sense of peace and comfort each day. Moreover, if you seek His help, the Lord can also assist you in developing new friendships, improving current relationships, repairing damaged relationships, and healing from the effects of painful interactions in the past.

Your closeness to and love for God and your efforts to serve Him, will help you to experience greater love and connection with others. This will happen as the Holy Ghost begins to change your heart through the Atonement of Jesus Christ, helping you to become more like the Savior, full of love for God and His children. As the prophet Moroni explained, "Wherefore, my beloved brethren, pray unto the Father with all the energy of heart, that ye may be filled with this love, which he hath bestowed upon all who are true followers of his Son, Jesus Christ; that ye may become the sons of God; that when he shall appear we shall be like him, for we shall see him as he is; that we may have this hope; that we may be purified even as he is pure. Amen."[16]

References to Chapter 6

1   Dieter F. Uchtdorf, "Of Regrets and Resolutions," *Ensign*, November 2012.

2   See "The Family: A Proclamation to the World," https://www.churchofje-suschrist.org/study/scriptures/the-family-a-proclamation-to-the-world/the-family-a-proclamation-to-the-world?lang=eng and D&C 131:1–4.

3   See "The Family: A Proclamation to the World," https://www.churchofje-suschrist.org/study/scriptures/the-family-a-proclamation-to-the-world/the-family-a-proclamation-to-the-world?lang=eng

4   *Teachings of the Prophet Joseph Smith*, sel. Joseph Fielding Smith (1976), 316.

5   D&C 130:2

6   Douglas Davies, *Child Development: A Practitioners Guide*, (New York: Guilford, 2011), 7–37.

7   Claudia Wallis, "The New Science of Happiness," *Time Magazine*, January 9, 2005; Kasley Killam, "To Combat Loneliness, Promote Social Health, *Scientific American*, January 23, 2018, https://www.scientificamerican.com/article/to-combat-loneliness-promote-social-health1/

8   Robert Waldinger, "What makes a good life? Lessons from the longest study on happiness," TED talk, November 2015. https://www.ted.com/talks/robert_waldinger_what_makes_a_good_life_lessons_from_the_longest_study_on_happiness?language=en

9   Holt-Lunstad J, Smith TB, Layton JB, "Social Relationships and Mortality Risk: A Meta-analytic Review," *PLoS Med* 7(7) (2010): https://doi.org/10.1371/journal.pmed.1000316).

10   See https://www.ncbi.nlm.nih.gov/pmc/articles/PMC7405486/

11   See https://www.cigna.com/about-us/newsroom/studies-and-reports/combatting-loneliness/

12   Holt-Lunstad, J.,Ibid; John Cacioppo and William Patrick, *Loneliness: Human Nature and the Need for Social Connection*, (New York: WW Norton, 2008), 5.

13   Dieter F. Uchtdorf, "Of Regrets and Resolutions," *Ensign*, November 2012.

14   Ezra Taft Benson, "Beware of Pride," *Ensign*, May 1989.

15   Linda K. Burton, "We'll Ascend Together," *Ensign*, May 2015.

16   Moroni 7:48

Chapter 7

ACQUIRING SELF-COMPASSION AND QUIETING THE INNER CRITIC

If your compassion does not include yourself, it is incomplete.

—Jack Kornfield [1]

ONE OF THE capacities that humans possess is the ability to think critically. This is an important skill that enables us to evaluate situations and options, look at the evidence, see things clearly, and make good decisions. It is also necessary for self-improvement in that we need to be able to examine ourselves with a critical eye to see our mistakes, faults, and weaknesses and envision pathways for making improvements.

The problem, however, is that we often think too critically about our faults and engage in severe judgments of our performance without separating our behavior from our identity. Consequently, we can be disdainful, harsh, and unforgiving with ourselves for falling short, making mistakes, and having weaknesses. This stance toward ourselves is noticeably lacking in empathy and compassion and there is little appreciation for our humanness, individuality, and associated imperfections. As a result, we are burdened by feelings of shame, guilt, and inadequacy, and we question our abilities and our worthiness.

The other response we often have when we fall short is self-isolation. We pull away from others and feel that we are not worthy or fit to be around our associates due to our self-contempt and feelings of shame. This is usually associated with internal narratives about how bad we are and why we have failed or made a particular mistake.

There are various ways of trying to deal with this tormenting "internal critic," including pushing yourself even harder to achieve and perform, distracting yourself by constantly staying busy, attempting to counteract the critical voice by seeking affirmation and acceptance from others, or retreating into substance use, compulsive eating, technology, pornography, or other addictions. Of course, these efforts at coping fall short of the goal and usually cause significant stress, anxiety and unhappiness.

Ted had a client who was constantly engaged in trying to achieve a goal or accomplish some worthwhile task. While his efforts to do worthwhile things lead to accomplishments that were laudable and praised by others, he actually got little real joy and satisfaction from his achievements. His problem was that once he attained his goal, he would not allow himself to stop and enjoy what he had done. Instead, he would quickly focus on the next task, which he compulsively pursued. Psychologically, his workaholic style of life was an effort to ward off self-critical and self-disparaging thoughts, such as "you are not worthy to be happy," that were tormenting him. Were he to let himself slow down and move away from his obsession with accomplishment, he would have become depressed and a victim to his self-punitive inner critic.

Enter Self-Compassion

An alternative approach to evaluating ourselves, is to view our mistakes and weaknesses through an eye of understanding and compassion. Compassion can be defined as concern or sympathy for the suffering of others, and is often associated with a desire to alleviate the suffering. Self-compassion entails an attitude of kindness, concern, caring and support for oneself when we confront personal inadequacies or situational difficulties. It is treating yourself as an ally and a friend, rather than an enemy. It is especially important when we suffer—whether it is the result of our own mistakes or the actions of others, or related to losses, failures or other disappointments.

Just as we all suffer, we all have the capacity for compassion. It is a part of our humanness. Research in neurobiology informs us that there are three broad motivational systems in humans.[2] The first is the fight or flight system, which is activated when we feel threat or danger and is designed for protection and safety. When this system is activated, adrenaline and cortisol are produced and we either fight, flee or freeze. The feelings involved are usually anxiety and anger. This system is activated when we sense danger, including being attacked physically or emotionally, either by others or ourselves. Persistent self-criticism can also activate this system, which over time may lead to chronic anxiety and depression.

The second system is the achievement and goal-seeking system which has to do with our drive for accomplishment. It is activated when we are engaged in achieving or obtaining something desirable and involves the neurotransmitter dopamine. This system is associated with feelings of interest and excitement.

The third system is the attachment, or the "tend and befriend" system, which has to do with our desires for connection and safety. This system is associated with the neurotransmitter oxytocin, which produces feelings of soothing, contentment, and well-being. It is within this system that we experience feelings of compassion for others and ourselves. Interestingly, recent research evidence indicates that self-compassion may trigger the release of oxytocin in the body.[3]

The gospel of Jesus Christ teaches us that compassion is an attribute of Godliness that is closely associated with charity and is a desired virtue of the Disciples of Christ.[4] While compassion and kindness toward others is a personal quality that we are taught to develop in our growing-up years and that we intrinsically value, compassion for self is not taught as a virtue and can be difficult to justify. For many of us, self-compassion may seem like a form of selfishness, self-pity, or self-indulgence because we are so used to pushing ourselves, ignoring our feelings, and criticizing our performance. When things go wrong and we become aware of our frustration and emotional pain, it is easy to be contemptuous with ourselves for having such feelings. "Just suck it up," "quit whining," or "others are much worse off than you," are examples of internal scolding that might occur if we allow ourselves to think to deeply about how we feel.

A twenty-five-year-old man was having trouble sleeping at night. In fact, it was not uncommon for him to stay up all night because he could not go to sleep. As he talked further about his situation, it became clear that stress, anxiety, and depression were a big part of his inability to sleep. At one point he confessed, "I feel embarrassed coming in here and talking about this stuff. Yes, I don't sleep well and I am probably depressed, but there are so many other people who have much bigger problems. I just need to quit complaining, suck it up, and get over myself."

Interestingly, research on self-compassion indicates that it is not associated with narcissism or selfishness, but with stable feelings of self-worth.[5] Moreover, those who practice self-compassion are more likely to focus on the needs and feelings of others and take more responsibility for their own feelings and behavior.[6]

The Core Components of Self-Compassion

Self-compassion entails three core components. The first is mindfulness, which means being aware of our moment-to-moment experience, especially our painful emotions and thoughts. Second is self-kindness, which is having an understanding and gentle attitude toward ourselves instead of harsh self-criticism and judgment. And third is a sense of common humanity, which involves the understanding that we can feel connected to others in our life experiences and do not have to struggle and suffer in isolation.

Mindfulness. Developing a greater degree of self-acceptance and compassion first requires an awareness of and an openness to how we might be feeling at any given moment. This is not an easy thing to do because most of us spend our time operating in the reacting/pushing mode of existence, where the focus is on action and problem solving. We get so wrapped up in our thoughts that we do not notice how we feel, particularly if it involves painful emotions such as disappointment, sadness, hurt, shame, or guilt. Lack of awareness of our feelings leaves us in a position of having our mental states and our behavior influenced in a significant way by feelings that we only dimly understand.

On the other hand, as we become more skilled at noticing our emotions we can then reflect on what they are, why they are there, what meanings they have and how they influence us. This process is succinctly described in the phrase "You can't heal what you can't feel."

Take, for example, a woman who wakes up feeling somewhat down and irritable and goes through the day in a sour mood. During the course of the day, she chides herself for not feeling more happy and upbeat, particularly since this was an exciting time in their family as their oldest son just three days earlier had received his mission call to South America. There was a large family gathering for the event (pre-pandemic), and everyone was excited when he opened his call and announced he would be serving in Peru.

Amidst chiding herself for not feeling better, this woman was probably unaware that her son's mission call may have triggered other feelings in her, perhaps painful feelings, that she was unaware of and unable to see how they were influencing her. Specifically, there is a strong possibility that she was feeling sadness and a sense of loss as she anticipated her son's departure. There may have also been some underlying feelings of resentment that the Church was taking her son away for two years, and she would have limited contact with him. In response to these feelings, she may have felt guilty and shameful for reacting in a way that she thought was selfish.

Had she been more aware of her feelings, she would have had the opportunity to make the connection between them and her sour mood. This would have opened up the option of being more accepting and compassionate toward herself and exploring why she had the feelings she did and what, if anything, she wanted to do about them.

Becoming more aware of your emotions is not an easy task since we all usually spend much mental energy trying to hide or ignore emotions that are uncomfortable or seem unacceptable. However, adopting a stance of curiosity about your feelings and taking time to ponder and reflect on them can be healthy and productive. You can also develop an accepting attitude toward your feelings, keeping in mind that feelings are neither good nor bad in and of themselves, they just are. Feelings are also different from behavior. Feelings may lead to behavior, which could be good or bad; however, what you feel is very different from what you do. Your sensitivity to emotions can also be enhanced by the Holy Ghost as you prayerfully ponder and seek the Lord's guidance (see D&C 9:8).

While awareness and acceptance of our experience is essential for self-compassion, it is also important that we do not become overly identified with our negative thoughts and define ourselves by our flaws and failures. For example, "I felt worthless in that situation" is much different than "I am a worthless person," or "I felt bad for what I said last night," is not the same as "I am an inconsiderate person."

Self-Kindness. Once you improve your ability to notice how you feel, then you can start considering your attitudes toward your feelings. As alluded to above, our default mode in dealing with ourselves is often one of judgment and criticism. Most of us seem to have little tolerance for our suffering, our struggles, and our weaknesses, and we often view these human frailties through the lens of self-contempt. As an alternative, we can work on developing within ourselves a voice of empathy and kindness that leads to greater understanding of our mistakes and shortcomings and less condemning of ourselves. As we consistently focus on trying to treat ourselves with greater kindness, we can eventually transform our critical internal appraisals into an internal dialogue that is more accepting, gentle, and compassionate toward ourselves. We can learn to talk to ourselves like a good friend.

One of our clients, who had suffered a great deal because of castigating himself mercilessly for his flaws, gradually began to develop an inner voice of compassion that helped him respond to his mistakes and shortcomings with more understanding and kindness. This change allowed him to become more tolerant of his weaknesses and to reflect upon and process other feelings that he had blocked out, such as sadness and shame. Not only did this help him feel better, but he noticed that he was also beginning to deal with others in a more open and understanding way.

It is important to note that the goal of self-compassion is not to take away or get rid of the painful feelings we are experiencing but to provide a sense of comfort and soothing in the midst of pain. This gives us confidence that whatever we are experiencing can be faced, tolerated, and accepted with the ongoing inner assurance that we will be able to deal with it. In addition, having compassion toward ourselves can help us realize that while we may not be totally responsible for the problems and pain we experience, we are responsible for what we do about it, and the first step is to treat ourselves in a kind and patient way.

Common Humanity. As you work to develop greater compassion in response to your inadequacies and faults, you will come to realize that you are not alone in your suffering. Indeed, you are part of a vast family of our Heavenly Father's children, each of whom, at times, also falls short, makes mistakes, and suffers. Suffering, in whatever form it takes, is part of the human experience that needs to be accepted and embraced. It is through the acknowledgment of suffering that we develop a greater capacity for compassion for self and others and a stronger sense of connection with the people around us.

Our sense of interconnectedness in our suffering helps us to feel less isolated and enables us to appreciate that we have much in common with the people around us; that we are all in this together, and share many of the same experiences and feelings, such as disappointment and weakness. In essence, it is the understanding that the pain we feel is essentially the same as others feel, even though the causes, circumstances and the degree of pain may be different. This understanding helps to sustain us at those times when we feel that we are unique in our flaws and our suffering.

Part of our work as mental health professionals involves conducting group therapy. One important aspect of group therapy is called *universality*, which is essentially the realization among group members that their problems are not unique to themselves but are shared by other group members. Understanding that they are not alone in their struggles and that others suffer from the same maladies as they do, is a powerful factor in helping them to feel better about themselves and more connected to both the people in the group and those in their lives generally.

Accepting our humanness and our propensity to fall short is not only therapeutic but opens up the possibility of change and growth. Self-compassion creates a safe space where an individual can look honestly at themselves and have confidence that mistakes and failures will be viewed from a perspective of kindness and understanding. While it is true that we all need to evaluate our performance to become aware of areas that need improvement, there is an important difference between a compassionate personal assessment or inspired self-evaluation[7] that is used to facilitate improvement, and an evaluation of self that is laced with attitudes of self-contempt and deprecation.

Moreover, some people believe that if they do not criticize themselves they will lose motivation for change and never improve or progress. One of our clients admitted that he was hesitant to become less self-critical and more self-compassionate because he was afraid of losing his edge in the business world and would, therefore, not push himself hard enough to continue to enjoy the level of success he had previously achieved. Ironically for my client, research studies indicate that individuals with higher levels of self-compassion also exhibit higher levels of motivation and self-confidence.[8]

Self-criticism makes it hard to improve because being honest with oneself about missteps, sins, and weaknesses is associated with painful feelings of shame and self-contempt. Our natural response to this is to hide and deny, which interferes with our motivation for self-examination and efforts to change. On the other hand, when you are kind to yourself, you see yourself more clearly, and it is easier to contemplate change, develop objectives, and experiment with how to do it. It also makes it okay if you struggle and do not succeed immediately.

With an attitude of acceptance toward self, individuals have more freedom from urges to compare themselves with others in an effort to feel better. Moreover, your sense of worth is not just based on successes and accomplishments but a stronger sense of intrinsic value based on common humanity and an understanding of our familial connection to our Heavenly Father, a connection which endows us with inherited worth and divine potential. While self-criticism creates anxiety and self-doubt, self-compassion leads to hope and confidence.

How Much Self-Compassion Do You Have?

At this point you might be wondering about how you are doing when it comes to self-compassion—how you respond to yourself when things go wrong. Dr. Kristin Neff at the University of Texas has developed a test that is useful in assessing this quality. For a snapshot of where you are, go to self-compassion.org, a website developed by Dr. Neff, and take a quick, twenty-five question test that will give you a rating of your level of self-compassion. If your score was high, you may not need to read the rest of this chapter. However, if you are like most of us, your ability to show compassion to yourself may need a little work.

Benefits of Self-Compassion

It is notable that the expanding research on self-compassion has revealed some valuable benefits. For example, self-compassion is associated with lower stress and better physical health, along with greater investment in general health promoting behaviors, including exercise, healthy eating and healthy sleeping. In fact, those who have more self-compassion also exhibit better coping and resilience in dealing with stress, lower levels of anxiety and depression, and less shame and self-criticism.[9]

For instance, the results of one study indicated that soldiers who had been in combat had less chance of developing PTSD if they had self-compassion.[10] Individuals who have self-compassion are also more optimistic, self-confident, and resilient and have higher levels of happiness and well-being.[11] Partners in romantic relationships who have self-compassion tend to be more caring and less controlling of their partner and exhibit higher levels of forgiveness, altruism, and empathy.[12] Even children and adolescents can become more self-compassionate, and those who can do that become more resilient and less impacted by life stresses, such as academic failure.[13]

Developing Self-Compassion

Developing self-compassion is a process that will require time, effort, and patience. It will also involve a shift from contempt and criticism to understanding and acceptance. There are also some specific strategies that, if implemented, can help. (For a broader and more elaborated description of strategies for improving self-compassion, see books by Kristin Neff and Christopher Germer.[14])

1. Changing your internal critic. The first place to start in cultivating self-compassion is to modify your critical self-talk. We all have internal dialogues that are essentially a running commentary about ourselves—our experiences and our behavior. Too often, that commentary is negative and critical in nature. The first step toward changing this type of self-talk is to notice when you are being self-critical. This involves paying attention to the unkind and harsh words and phrases that you repeat to yourself that are often habitual and may be out of your awareness. When you are feeling bad, try to think about what you have been saying to yourself, noting the actual words as well as the attitude and tone of voice of your internal critic. In fact, you may wish to record these criticisms to become more aware of them.

For example, a father might disdainfully say to himself, "it was childish of you to get upset and yell at Jimmy (his son)." If this man was able to notice his critical self-talk, he could replace the dialogue with words that were more kind and understanding. His response to himself might have been, "I got frustrated and lost patience when I was trying to teach him the rules of the game. I don't like it when I do that, but it is not going to help to beat myself up for it. I just need to work on calming myself before I lose my cool." Other examples of kinder self-talk in everyday life are "It's okay to make a mistake," "It is not weak to admit that my feelings were hurt," and "It is all right to struggle when things are hard."

Consider the following situation that many of us have encountered: You realize as you are pulling out of the driveway that you forgot to fill your car with gas last evening, and now the gas gauge is sitting on "empty." Your first inclination might be to think, "I can't believe I forgot to get gas; that was so stupid of me." Once you realize what you are doing, you could stop yourself and think of kinder and equally realistic words to use, such as, "I can't believe I forgot to get gas; I guess I was pretty tired last night," or "I probably just had too much on my mind." Using these phrases does not abrogate one from the responsibility of getting gas, but is a more supportive and understanding way to deal with yourself about the problem.

In developing and implementing a kinder vocabulary, you will naturally run into resistance from the part of your mind that is used to being critical. The critical voices will need to be consistently challenged over time and replaced with a more reasonable voice of tolerance for progress to be made. Some of the voices of contempt might even be familiar, such as the voice of a parent. As you learn to distinguish those voices from your newer, kinder voice, it is easier to minimize and discard them.

2. Treating yourself as you would a friend. Another helpful approach to developing self-compassion is to try to respond to yourself in the same way that you would respond to a friend who was struggling with self-criticism. Think of some aspect of your personality or behavior for which you feel shame, disappointment, or discontent. Then imagine that instead of you, it is your friend who has these problems. Consider how you would communicate to your friend about their problem, and then write a letter to him or her, summarizing your thoughts. Try to apply the same words of compassion and encouragement to yourself.

As an example, a client once told Ted how upset and angry she was at herself after losing track of her children at a city park while engrossed in a conversation with a friend whom she had not seen in some time. In describing the situation, she was rather harsh in her language, describing herself as irresponsible, neglectful and self-absorbed.

Ted suggested that she think about how she would talk to a good friend if they had done the same thing she did. After thinking about it for a few seconds, she said that she would probably tell her friend that she was being too hard on herself and, instead of referring to herself as irresponsible and neglectful, it might be more accurate to say that she simply became distracted for a brief period. She related further that she would tell her friend that instead of characterizing herself as self-absorbed, it would be more accurate to say that that she temporarily lost her focus on her children because she was so happy to see the other woman. In her explanation of what happened, this woman focused more on her friend's behavior than on her character. Furthermore, she described the loss of focus on her children as a temporary event, not a personal style.

Another approach could be to write a letter to *yourself* each day for seven days from the perspective of a person who is a good friend to you. Choose something about yourself that causes you to feel shame, insecurity, or inadequacy. It might be something about your physical appearance or a character flaw or a weakness. Write a short, one-paragraph letter to yourself from the perspective of your friend, addressing your flaw. In the letter, describe how your friend would react to your flaw, what he or she would say about it, and what changes your friend would recommend you make. Do this for seven consecutive days and see if it makes a difference in how you view your flaws and weaknesses.

Writing a compassionate letter to yourself each day might be difficult to do initially because it is so different from how we usually talk to ourselves and may even seem to be overindulgent. However, those who diligently write a letter each day usually find that their attitudes toward themselves begin to change—they are more in tune with their personal struggles and have a more realistic and tolerant view of themselves.

In thinking about this kind of a friend, perhaps you thought about the Savior. How would he respond to you? There are many examples in the scriptures depicting the compassionate way Christ responded to people who made mistakes, committed sins, and struggled with shortcomings. One of the poignant examples was the woman taken in adultery (See John 8:3–11). After convicting the accusing Jews with his incisive injunction, "he that is without sin, let him first cast a stone," Jesus turned to the woman and asked, "woman, where are thine accusers?" She responded by stating that they were gone. Then Jesus stated, "Neither do I accuse thee, go and sin no more." He did not say that what she did was acceptable but indicated, without accusing, condemning, or judging her that she needed to change her behavior. The Savior would most assuredly extend the same level of love and non-judgmental acceptance to each of us.

Jesus is not a harsh, critical judge, as we often are with ourselves, but is an understanding, compassionate friend, who is interested in loving and helping us. When Christ appeared to the people in ancient America, one of the first things he did was to heal their sick and afflicted and blessed their children. While He was engaged in this, Jesus twice stated that he had *compassion* for all the people who were there (see 3 Nephi 17:6–7).

3. Keep a self-compassion journal. Another helpful exercise is to keep a self-compassion journal. Writing in a journal is a good way to organize your experiences and express emotions and is associated with considerable therapeutic benefit. Perhaps the best way to do this is to take a few minutes at the end of each day to write down your experiences of the day, taking note to write about anything that caused you to feel bad about yourself or to judge or criticize yourself. For each experience, first write what happened, how you felt about the situation, and what kinds of self-judgments and self-criticisms were present.

Next, write down how your feelings or behaviors were connected to the larger human experience, meaning how it was not so different from what many of us feel or do. Remembering that all of us are imperfect and make mistakes, for example. Thinking about the reasons you did what you did and all the factors involved in it would also be helpful. For example, "I was already upset because we were running late to the appointment." Lastly, write some words to yourself that convey kindness and comfort, such as "You didn't do too well, but it's going to be okay," "Most everyone does that at times," or "Sometimes things just build up, and you overreact."

4. Facing current pain. You can practice self-compassion by thinking about something in your life that is causing you emotional pain. Think of who is involved, when it happens, and what is causing the discomfort. Think also about the kinds of feelings you are having, such as anger, sadness, disappointment, or fear. Then try to generate some phrases that you can use and perhaps repeat to yourself to help you to acknowledge and face the pain and to comfort and sooth yourself. Such phrases could include "This is really hard" or "I'm struggling with this." Additional phrases could be, "Remember, suffering is a part of life and the Lord's plan, and he will help me through it," or "I'm not alone in my suffering; others feel like I do," and "the Savior understands how I feel and will comfort me." Through this process, it is helpful to remember that when we acknowledge and experience our painful feelings, they eventually transform and become easier to bear.

5. Feeling the Savior's compassion. Your ability to be compassionate toward yourself and others is greatly enhanced when you feel the Savior's love and compassion for you. The scriptures teach us, "God is love," and that there is nothing that can separate us from His love (see Romans 8:38–39). As Elder Jeffrey R. Holland has described it, "My brothers and sisters, the first great commandment of all eternity is to love God with all of our heart, might, mind, and strength—that's the first great commandment. But the first great truth of all eternity is that God loves us with all of His heart, might, mind, and strength. That love is the foundation stone of eternity, and it should be the foundation stone of our daily life."[15]

If you are not sure how our Heavenly Father and Jesus Christ feel about you, the most direct way to find out is to ask. Remember the great truth in the New Testament: "Ask, and it shall be given unto you" (Matthew 7:7). The answer may not come immediately or in a way you expected, but it will come, and it can forever change the way you feel about yourself. As M. Russell Ballard has stated, *One of the sweetest messages the Spirit will relay is how the Lord feels about you.*"[16]

Because of his love for us, the Savior took upon himself and experienced the kinds of pain and suffering that we experience. Alma taught that the Savior suffered "pains and afflictions and temptations of every kind" and took upon him the pains and sicknesses of his people, so that he may know according to the flesh how to succor his people (See Alma 7:11–12).

Elaborating on this doctrine, Elder Neal A. Maxwell explained,

Jesus' perfect empathy was ensured when, along with His Atonement for our sins, He took upon Himself our sicknesses, sorrows, griefs, and infirmities and came to know these "according to the flesh" (Alma 7:11–12). He did this in order that He might be filled with perfect, personal mercy and empathy and thereby know how to succor us in our infirmities. He thus fully comprehends human suffering. Truly Christ "descended below all things, in that He comprehended all things" (D&C 88:6).

. . . Jesus Christ, who by far suffered the most, has the most compassion—for all of us who suffer so much less."[17]

The Savior desires for us to feel his love and compassion and extends it to us if we desire it and ask for it. Emulating and adopting as our own his attitude toward us, especially when we have fallen short, made mistakes and committed sins, would be a big step toward developing a more compassionate, less critical and more realistic inner voice.

Consistent efforts to respond to ourselves with compassion as we deal with the struggles of daily life, and with our own inadequacies and mistakes can lessen our suffering, increase our capacity to cope, and enhance feelings of peace and well-being. It will also help us to understand and compassionately respond to others who are also struggling and suffering. Through this process, we become more charitable, loving, and kind; more able to serve others; and more like Jesus, the perfect example of compassion.

References to Chapter 7

1   Jack Kornfield, *Buddha's Little Instruction Book* (New York: Bantam Books, 1994).

2   Kristin Neff, *Self-Compassion* (New York: Harper Collins, 2011), Chapter 3.

3   Neff.

4   "Charity," Gospel Topics, churchofjesuschrist.org/topics.

5   Kristen Neff & Roos Vonk, "Self—Compassion vs. Global Self-Esteem: Two Different Ways of Relating to Oneself," *Journal of Personality* (2009), 77, 23–50.

6   Kristen Neff & S. Natasha Beretvas, "The Role of Self-Compassion in Romantic Relationships," *Self and Identity,* (2012), 1–21.

7   Dallin Oaks, "Small and Simple Things," *Ensign*, May 2018.

8   Juliana G. Breines & Serena Chen, "Self-compassion Increases Self-Improvement Motivation," *Personality and Social Psychology Bulletin*, May 29, 2012.

9   Kristen Neff, Stephanie S. Rude and Kristen L. Kirkpatrick, "An examination of self-compassion in relation to positive psychological functioning and personality traits," *Journal of Research in Personality*, 2007, 41, 908–916.; Kristen Neff, "Self-Compassion," in *Handbook of Individual Differences in Social Behavior*, ed. Mark R. Leary and Rick H. Hoyle (NY: Guilford Press, 2009), 561–573.

10 Katherine a Dahm, Eric Meyer, Kristen Neff, Nathan Kimbrel, Suzy Bird Gulliver, and Sandra Morissette, "Mindfulness, self-compassion, post-traumatic stress disorder symptoms and functional disability in US, Iraq and Afghanistan war veterans," *Journal of Traumatic Stress* (2015), 1–5.

11 Laura K. Barnard and John Curry, "Self-compassion: Conceptualizations, Correlates and Interventions," *Review of General Psychology* (2011) 15, 289–303.

12 Kristen Neff & S. Natasha Beretvas, "The Role of Self-Compassion in Romantic Relationships," *Self and Identity* (2012), 1–21.

13 Kristen Neff and Pittman McGehee, "Self-Compassion and Psychological Resilience Among Adolescents and Young Adults," *Self and Identity*, 2010, 9, 225–240.)

14 Neff, *Self-Compassion*; Kristin Neff & Christopher Germer, *The Mindful Self-Compassion Workbook: A Proven Way to Accept Yourself, Build Inner Strength, and Thrive* (New York: Guilford, 2018).

15 Jeffrey R. Holland, "Tomorrow the Lord will Work Wonders Among You," *Ensign*, May 2016.

16 M. Russell Ballard, "Women of Righteousness," *Ensign*, April 2002.

17 Neal A. Maxwell, "Enduring Well," *Ensign*, May 1997.

Chapter 8

STAYING ON TOP OF STRESS

Stress is like spice—in the right proportion it enhances the flavor of a dish. Too little produces a bland, dull meal; too much may choke you.

—Donald Tubesing[1]

ONCE AGAIN, JOHN is lying awake at 4:00 a.m. although he desperately wishes that he could fall back to sleep. The seminary class he teaches begins at 6:00 a.m., but he believes he can easily make it if he wakes up at 5:00. Instead, his mind is racing, focused on everything that has to be done that day after seminary: another packed day of projects and meetings at work, a noon appointment with an insurance agent, a committee meeting at the school in the early evening followed by a ministering appointment. As he ponders over these matters in the early dawn hours, his attention then shifts to the heated discussion with his sixteen-year-old son the night before. John is quite concerned about how much time his son is spending with his girlfriend. John is also surprised at how upset and angry he has become with his son. Concerns about money suddenly intrude themselves into his thought process along with an awareness of his growing resentment about the financial demands he has to contend with daily. As his wife, Jill, turns over in bed, he wonders, "With all that is going on will we be able to have dinner as a family? What about working out?" John lets out a frustrated sigh as he realizes there will not be time for either one on this particular day.

Does this scenario sound familiar? In our counseling work, we have met many active and faithful Latter-day Saints who lead very busy lives, filled with good and necessary things, but who are also experiencing the negative effects of too much stress. Even though the Lord has counseled us that "it is not requisite that a man should run faster than he has strength" (Mosiah 4:27) we often feel that "running faster" is exactly what we must do each day. Do you have trouble sleeping at night because of worries and tension? Do you find yourself being impatient and snappy with co-workers and family members? Are you bothered by consistent headaches, fatigue or stomach problems? These are a few of the symptoms you might experience when your stress level becomes too high.

We live in a society that is efficient at generating stress and most of us are affected in one way or another. Research studies indicate that over 80 percent of visits to doctors' offices are for stress-related disorders.[2] In addition, recent surveys by the American Psychological Association indicate that most Americans are suffering from at least moderate levels of stress, with one fourth reporting that they experience extreme levels of stress. More than three-quarters of adults report physical or emotional symptoms of stress, such as headaches, feeling tired, or changes in sleeping habits. Moreover, nearly half of Americans report lying awake at night because of stress and one-third report feeling anxious, irritable and fatigued. Results from the studies we are citing further suggested that chronic stress—the kind that interferes with your ability to function normally day to day—is becoming "a public health crisis."[3]

More recently, the COVID-19 pandemic has caused an upsurge in stress levels among Americans, and in 2020 the average reported stress level was higher than at any time since 2007, when the American Psychological Association began conducting stress surveys.[4] The major stressors related to COVID-19 were fears of getting sick; work and financial concerns; disrupted routines; isolation; managing education/distance learning for kids; maintaining access to food, housing, and healthcare; and missing out on milestones, such as graduations. Parents were experiencing significantly more stress than non-parents due to challenges in having children at home all day, managing routines, and taking care of school and online learning.

Good and Bad Stress

Stress is our body's reaction to the threats and demands we experience and is something we must face almost daily. We usually think about stress in negative terms, as an unwanted commodity intruding into our lives and disrupting our equanimity. To be sure, stress, especially when it is ongoing or repeated, can wreak havoc with our existence, making us physically sick and spiritually and emotionally compromised. Stress suppresses the immune system, disrupts sleep and contributes to heart disease. Moreover, stress also creates anxiety and tension, can trigger depression, and even affects memory loss.

It may be surprising then, to learn that stress can also be an ally, a motivating force for action and achievement. Stress can infuse us with energy to complete the project, take one more run down a steep ski slope, face an intimidating boss, or deal with a painful medical procedure. In the right amount, stress can be the stimulation that helps us to keep moving forward, facing challenges and experiencing the consequent expansion of our capabilities. In fact, the results of a recent study scientifically validated the often heard expression that "whatever doesn't kill you makes you stronger" if it is experienced at manageable levels.[5]

The relationship between stress and performance can be understood using the "Yerkes-Dodson Curve" which is named after two Harvard scientists who found that as stress levels increase, so does performance—up to a certain point.[6] Specifically, as shown in this figure, (which appears on the next page) when you are feeling little stress (you are bored or uninterested for example), then performance levels are typically low because it is hard to muster up the wherewithal, drive, and motivation to perform well. When stress levels land in the moderate range, stress is energizing and you perform successfully and excel. Finally, performance begins to diminish as your stress climbs higher and becomes impaired as your body is increasingly overtaxed because of too much stress.

YERKES-DODSON CURVE

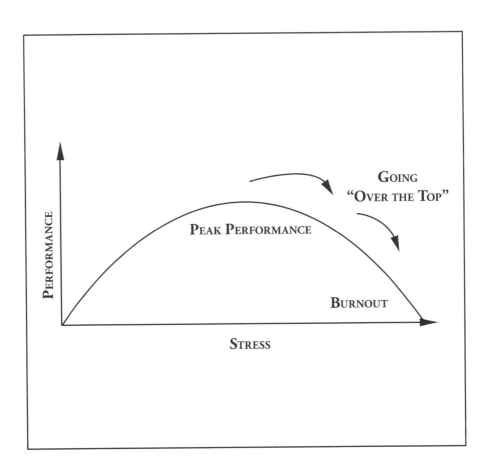

Our goal in dealing with stress is not to avoid or alleviate all stress but to find the middle point, the moderate level, where stress is experienced more as a challenge rather than a threat. At this level, performance can be optimized.

How Stressed Are You?

When we become stressed, our brain responds by engaging the sympathetic (fight or flight) nervous system and releasing specific stress hormones (i.e., adrenaline, noradrenaline and cortisol). As these hormones are released into our blood stream, we are now better equipped to deal with the challenge by increasing our heart rate, our breathing rate, and our blood flow. This process intensifies our alertness and physical energy. In the short run we benefit from this process and our performance is enhanced, whether we are taking a test, giving a presentation, or confronting a tiger in the jungle. However, if your sympathetic nervous system is stuck in the on position because of unremitting stress, then the fight or flight response and related stress hormones turn from being a helpful friend to a damaging enemy that can hurt both your mind and body.

When your fight or flight system is engaging too often or too long, then you are experiencing overstress or "toxic stress," the kind of stress that erodes physical, mental, emotional, and spiritual strength. In some instances, overstress is easy to recognize as in the opening story about John where someone is clearly overwhelmed by a situation. On the other hand, many people who are chronically overstressed are unaware or only dimly aware of how stressed they really are and the toll it is taking on them. It is only when they receive a message from their body in the form of a bothersome physical symptom—ongoing stomach problems, headaches, or fatigue—or hear a comment about their behavior from someone close to them, such as, "you are always so grumpy and on edge these days," that they pause long enough to consider that life may not be going well. Even when it becomes clear that something is wrong, we may not have much of a clue as to what is causing the problem and what role stress is playing.

For example, a bishop shared with us the following experience. He was bogged down with many serious problems that members of his ward were encountering. At the same time, he was running his own business, which was doing well, but the work was quite overwhelming. On a particular evening, he walked into his local chapel where a wedding reception was being held. One of the first members of his ward that he met said, "Bishop, you look terrible. Are you okay?" The ward member, whom the bishop considered a wise woman because of the many trying experiences she had been through, advised the bishop that he should visit the doctor—for at least a check-up. The bishop followed the counsel of the well-meaning ward member and discovered that he had high blood pressure—a condition caused by stress for sure. This particular bishop had no idea that the pressure he was under was taking a significant toll on his body.

Fortunately, there are indicators that can help you determine when the stress has become too much. These "red flags" include physical, emotional, behavioral, and spiritual markers that can alert you that it is time to take a look at what is going on and consider making a course correction. Below is a partial list of common indicators of overstress.

- *Physical Symptoms:* tension, headaches, upset stomach, indigestion, loss of appetite, fatigue, sore muscles, and frequent illnesses
- *Emotional/Mental Symptoms:* irritability, impatience, anxiety, depression, concentration problems, feeling overwhelmed, anger, guilt, chronic worry, memory problems
- *Behavioral Symptoms:* overeating, increased caffeine use, decreased activity, lack of motivation, crying, interpersonal conflict, increased medication or substance use, sleeplessness
- *Spiritual Symptoms:* feeling disconnected to God and others, loss of interest in church calling and serving others, cynicism or indifference to leaders/programs/teachers, resentment about expectations and duties, feeling more vulnerable to temptation and sin, doubts about one's ability to live the gospel, consistent feelings of unworthiness

An honest evaluation of how stress is impacting you is the first step toward doing something about it. A simple way to assess your stress level is to read through the above listed stress symptoms and write down any that apply to you. If you are experiencing any of these symptoms, then honestly ask yourself if your current level of stress is causing you discomfort and having a negative impact on your life. If your answer is yes, then it is probably time to take a serious look at what is stressing you, where it is coming from, and what you can do about it.

Stress and Mental Health

Mild to moderate levels of stress can usually be controlled through the use of stress management strategies such as those described in this book. However, when stress is more severe and ongoing it can lead to the development of more serious mental health problems. For example, stress and anxiety often go together and both involve the "fight or flight" system. While stress triggers a response from your body to help you adapt to a threat or a demand, anxiety is a feeling of fear or apprehension resulting from a perception of threat or danger. High stress can result in debilitating levels of anxiety characterized by excessive or unreasonable fears or apprehension, excessive worry, panic attacks, irritability, loss of sleep, and phobias.

What Are Your Stressors?

Some stresses affect most of us to some degree and are easily identified, such as concerns about work, money, family responsibilities, relationships and our health. There are also major events that occur in life that are clearly recognized as very stressful. These include divorce, death of a loved one, job loss, experiencing a serious injury or illness, rape, abuse, being physically assaulted, and the recent COVID-19 pandemic, just to name a few.

Other stressors, however, are more subtle and hard to identify. For example, you may be only mildly aware of the nagging feeling of not ever having done enough, or you might be oblivious to the cumulative impact that seemingly small annoyances are having on you. You may also get caught in the trap of feeling like you have to do things perfectly, or perhaps you are prone to take on too much, or feel guilty if you say no to a request from another parent to help with a school event. Some of us believe that we are unworthy if we are not "anxiously engaged" in doing something productive at all times.

Another category of stressors that we may not actually perceive as stress producing are what might be termed "daily hassles." These are everyday experiences that consistently grind on us creating tension and anxiety and taxing our coping resources. These include being overloaded at work, a tough commute, not getting enough sleep, bothersome neighbors, disagreements at home, a never-ending stack of bills to pay, and having too many civic, school, and church responsibilities. There is a common misconception that stress is about big events like the death of a loved one or divorce. While these can be very stressful, they are usually time-limited and cause us to mobilize our coping resources to meet the challenge. On the other hand, there is research evidence indicating that daily hassles can have a stronger negative impact on our health than the big events.[7]

It might also come as a surprise to learn that stress often occurs on the heels of positive events. Getting married, graduating from college, and receiving a promotion at work are usually welcome happenings in our lives, but they can also create a good deal of stress. These kinds of stresses often go undetected and may lead to surprising feelings of anxiety and uneasiness. The effects of stress can also build upon itself. Moving to a new community, having a baby, and experiencing marital conflict all within the same year can cumulatively create enough stress to undermine your health, even if they occur months apart.

If you are unclear as to where your stress is coming from, you might try keeping a stress journal where you write down when you feel stressed and note the thoughts and feelings you are experiencing. Diligence in this process can reveal sources of daily stress that you may have overlooked or thought were insignificant. You might also make it a matter of prayer and seek the help of the Lord to better understand the stressors that impinge upon you.

How Do You Cope with Stress?

Just as we all have different thresholds for stress and are more affected by some stresses than others, we each have our own style of reacting to stress. Understanding how you respond to stress is useful because once you notice yourself feeling and behaving in ways that character-ize your style of reacting to stress, it is an early tip off that things are going awry and that something needs to change—either there needs to be a reduction in stress or a change in the way you are dealing with it. For example, you might find yourself being more easily irritated and moody at home, or you notice that you are having more difficulty concentrating and making decisions at work. An increase in the fre-quency of headaches or trouble falling or staying asleep might also be a signal that you are becoming overstressed.

As our stress level increases, we naturally marshal our resources to try and cope with the extra emotional load. Some of our coping strategies are effective and helpful; others are not and may even make things worse. If you respond to your stress signals by confronting the source of the stress and take steps to reduce or alleviate it, then you are responding in a healthy manner. In addition, running or riding a bike; venting or problem solving with family or friends; mediating and praying; and reading a book or watching your favorite TV pro-gram are all adaptive ways of dealing with stress.

On the other hand, if you deny that the stress exists or avoid deal-ing with it, then you are setting the stage for difficulties. Likewise, if you self-medicate by turning to "quick fixes" such as prescription medication, pornography, overeating, alcohol, spending sprees, and illegal drugs, you may experience temporary relief, but ultimately the situation will worsen. All of these behaviors create feelings of well-being and control, but the experience is illusory because once the effects wear off, then you are right back where you started.

For example, viewing pornography may result in an immediate release of tension and anxiety but afterward produces painful feelings of guilt, shame, and self-loathing that create even more stress. "Quick fixes" also encumber your efforts to deal with stress because they undermine your ability to recognize, understand and deal with what is bothering you, thus amplifying the deleterious effects of the original stressor. In essence, such quick fixes make a bad situation worse.

To help you determine your typical ways of coping with stress, write down on a piece of paper all of the ways you use to manage stress. Then go back and rate each one as either healthy or unhealthy. Healthy strategies are those that lead to long term reductions in stress.

Unhealthy strategies are those that seem to be effective in the short run but lead to increased stress later on.

If you find yourself using less healthy methods of dealing with stress, it may help to know that you are not alone. An interesting finding from the American Psychological Association survey previously described was that most Americans admitted that they were not doing a good job of taking care of themselves.[8] For instance, while 54 percent of respondents agreed that exercise was important, only 27 percent were happy about their own level of physical activity.

A classic example is Roger. A successful attorney with a bent toward perfectionism, he spends 10–12 hours a day at his job and often works on cases at home. In addition, he is the elders quorum president in his ward and coaches his son's soccer team. He tries to spend time with his family but notices that much of the time he is at home he would prefer just to watch TV or surf the internet while eating his favorite snack. If interrupted or presented with a problem by a family member, he is easily irritated and sometimes blows up. His wife has complained to him that he seems preoccupied and unavailable. When he is honest with himself, he admits that most of the time he feels edgy and would rather avoid interacting with others.

Roger's use of withdrawal, retreating into cyberspace, and overeating may calm his nerves partially, but he pays a price by creating bad feelings in his family and depriving himself of interactions with family members, particularly his wife, that might be helpful to him. At some point he will need to address the demands from work, his own driven nature, and his lack of helpful coping strategies. If he chooses to ignore the stress in his life, he runs the risk of becoming further detached from family members, developing physical symptoms, or gradually sinking into depression.

The Challenges and Benefits of Managing Stress

Once you recognize that overstress is a problem and you gain some awareness of where the stress is coming from, then you are in a position to do something about it. In most cases "doing something" means proactively changing the stressful situations you are in or doing something about the way you are coping with them. However, like most of us, you may not be willing to come to grips with reality and the impact stress is having on your life, and consequently, the lives of your family members. Questions that you might have about addressing the stress in your life might be: "Can I really do this?" "If so, what will it take to make it happen?" and "Will it just be more work for me?" The answers to these questions may only become clear once you try some of the suggestions and strategies discussed in the next chapter.

The key factor in whether you can make changes is not how hard it is or what exactly will be involved but how committed you are to doing it. To be committed you will have to resolve in your mind that the discomfort, pain, and turmoil that you are presently experiencing is no longer acceptable and that the potential benefits of tackling your stress problem are worth the effort.

In order to get to the point of seriously wanting to work on reducing your stress, you will also have to be willing to give up certain perceived benefits that stress affords you. For example, you might feel that stress is what energizes you and motivates you to accomplish. Or you might worry that you are going to have to start settling for something less than perfection if you lower your stress. For some, being "stressed out" is a badge of honor indicative of a hardworking and achievement oriented person. Evaluating and resolving these types of beliefs and concerns will be necessary before you will be able to fully focus your efforts on controlling your stress.

Excessive stress is a problem that each of us probably experiences to a greater or lesser degree. As you consider your stress level and what you want to do to about it, it is important to remember to start with making small and simple changes that will lead to incremental but meaningful changes in your stress level. This will result help you to feel a sense of success and stay motivated to continue in your efforts. In addition, and most importantly, remember that your Heavenly Father wants you to succeed and will give you divine help to assist if you ask for it. The Apostle Paul testified, "I can do all things through Christ which strengtheneth me" (Philippians 4:13). You have the same promise!

References to Chapter 8

1   See https://strathmore.edu/news/stress-is-like-spice/.

2   See Webmd.com/balance/stress-management.

3   American Psychological Association, "Stress in America," 2019, 2020; apa. org/stress.

4   APA, "Stress in America."

5   Seery, MD, Holman, EA, & Silver, RC., "Whatever Does Not Kill Us: Cumulative Life Adversity, Vulnerability, and Resilience, *Journal of Personality and Social Psychology,* 6, (2010), 1025–1041.

6   Yerkes, RM & Dodson, JD., "The Relation of Strength of Stimulus to Rapidity of Habit Formation. *Journal of Comparative Neurology and Psychology,* 18, (5) (1908), 459–482.

7   DeLongis, A, Folkman, S, & Lazarus, R. "The Impact of Daily Stress on Mood: Psychological and Social Resources as Mediators." *Journal of Personality and Social Psychology,* 54, no. 3 (1988), 486–495.

8   APA, "Stress in America."

Chapter 9

DE-STRESSING STRATEGIES

Rule number one is, don't sweat the small stuff.
Rule number two is, it's all small stuff.

—Robert Elliot [1]

As YOU GAIN a better understanding of how stress is affecting you, and the ways you have been trying to cope with it (helpful and unhelpful), you can begin developing stress management tools that are practical and work for you. Each chapter of this book contains suggestions that, while not specifically focused on stress, can help you to reduce stress, such as the suggestions on taking care of your body in later chapters. In this chapter we present a few specific methods that we think are useful, including avoiding stress when possible, finding ways to calm your mind, changing thinking patterns that promote stress, managing time, and acquiring practical problem-solving skills.

Sidestepping Stress

The first strategy in dealing with stress in simply trying to avoid or minimize stressful situations and events as much as possible. This usually takes some forethought and advanced planning about what kinds of stresses you may face at any particular time. Once you have made that determination, you can start thinking about how some stresses could be minimized or avoided altogether.

For example, suppose you are going to a meeting tomorrow morning at a location that is unfamiliar to you. You have the address and the directions, but if you take just a couple of minutes to plan the actual route you will be taking and check to see if there are likely to be any delays due to construction or congested traffic, you might end up modifying your route or at least being able to leave in enough time to keep from stressing about being late and arriving at the meeting in a state of frustration and anxiety.

Ted's wife told him on one occasion, "you create a lot of stress for yourself." After that pronouncement, the following ensued:

I immediately knew she was right, but I couldn't resist asking what she meant by that statement. She replied, "You are always rushing places because you try to fit in just a little more work or play before you leave, and you chronically underestimate the amount of time it takes to get places, and it stresses you out." As much as I did not like hearing it, what she said was true. I will also add that when I am in those situations, I am tense behind the wheel and have little patience for other drivers, especially slow drivers (usually old men with hats on). When I finally arrive at my destination, I am usually quite stressed and preoccupied with uncomfortable feelings of frustration and embarrassment about being late. At the same time, I am frantically engrossed in how I am going to explain my tardiness. In most cases, if I would have taken thirty to sixty seconds to think about where I was going, what time I needed to leave to be there, and planned out what I had time to do or not do before I left, I probably would have had a much more pleasant trip and could have avoided the stress and embarrassment of being late.

Many of us also have a propensity to take on more than we can reasonably manage without becoming unduly stressed. Before agreeing to accept a responsibility, such as a volunteer position in a professional group or a civic organization, it might be well to sit down and think about the actual time and work that would be involved and weigh that against the amount of time you actually have available and the likely amount of stress that might be associated with the responsibility. This would be especially important if you have trouble saying "No," or if you have a tendency to underestimate what might be required in time and energy to carry out a given task or responsibility.

Other examples might include avoiding a co-worker who emotionally dumps on you if you are available or a friend who is constantly asking you to watch her children. For men, what about the relative who is chronically down on his luck and needing to borrow money again, or parents who have an adult child who makes unreasonable demands on their time and money. In our Latter-day Saint culture, we often find ourselves volunteering to help and assist in areas when in actuality we do not have the time to take on such mammoth tasks. It is better to count the cost before we over commit ourselves, and then become resentful towards those who asked for our time in the first place.

Calming and Relaxing Your Mind and Body

Structured methods for relaxing and calming ourselves can add greatly to reducing the stress in our lives. For example, diaphragmatic breathing is an easy, portable way to relax your body and become calmer in almost any situation. When you breathe this way you experience decreased muscle tension, lower heartrate and lower blood pressure. The procedure is simple and involves inhaling deeply through your nose and letting your belly expand. The image of filling a balloon full of air in your stomach can sometimes be helpful. It is also useful to place one hand on your chest and the other on your stomach.

When you practice this technique, inhale through your nose and your stomach should expand while your chest stays still. Exhale through your mouth and notice that your belly falls. Many people find it helpful to count as they inhale and exhale. For example, while inhaling you can count "1-2-3-4," and while exhaling count just a little longer: "1-2-3-4-5." Just like any skill, it takes some time to get proficient at diaphragmatic breathing so it is important to practice it for five to ten minutes two to three times each day.

Mindful meditation has also become a popular way for people to relax and settle their minds. It can be described as awareness of present experience with acceptance. The benefits of this form of meditation have been well studied and include decreased stress, better immune functioning, less inflammation, greater self-acceptance, and overall awareness. It has been used successfully with stress reduction and treatment of anxiety, depression, and chronic pain.

The procedure for mindfulness meditation typically involves sitting in a comfortable position and focusing your attention on your breathing. This is followed by noticing bodily sensations, including noises, smells, and tactile experiences. Thoughts and feelings are also noticed and observed without getting entangled in them, which further promotes awareness and observation of the present. The idea is not to rid your mind of all thoughts, but to increase awareness and acceptance of your mental experience.

Some form of mindfulness meditation can be used in almost any situation and in small increments (two to three minutes). This can help settle an anxious or stressed mind and works best when practiced consistently. For beginners, it can be helpful to join a mindfulness group to learn the technique and to practice consistently. There are also several smart phone apps available that will take you through guided meditations including *Calm*, *HeadSpace*, *Mindfulness Coach*, and *Oak Meditation.*

Finally, consider progressive muscle relaxation. This is another widely used technique for reducing stress. It involves systematically tensing and relaxing the muscles in your body. It can be done while seated or lying on your back and proceeds by sequentially flexing the muscles in the various muscle groups of your body.

For example, you could start by flexing your biceps for ten seconds and then relaxing them for twenty seconds. This process helps you to notice the difference between tension and relaxation in your muscles while facilitating muscle relaxation. Furthermore, the process would continue by flexing and relaxing the muscles in your arms, legs, stomach, upper back, neck, shoulders, and head. The entire process can be completed in about ten minutes. An example of the progressive muscle technique can be found on *YouTube* under "Progressive Muscle Relaxation Training" by Mark Connelly from the Children's Mercy Hospital.

Modifying Stressful Thinking

The way we perceive and interpret what is happening around us has much to do with our experience of stress. As mentioned earlier, a moderate level of stress can be helpful to us because it increases our motivation and energizes us to face challenging situations. However, if we perceive a situation to be overly taxing and exceeding our capacity to effectively cope with it, then we feel threatened, overly stressed, and anxious.

For example, suppose you are going to give a presentation in front a group. If you are going over the key points of your presentation and have the subjective sense that, even though it is stressful, if you can face it and complete the task, then you are experiencing *challenge stress*. Individuals who experience this kind of stress often feel "pumped," and their bodies respond with directing blood to the brain and muscles to meet the challenge. Besides, if your hands are cold, your heart is racing, and you are so anxious and overwhelmed that you can't remember the points you want to make, then you are experiencing *threat stress*. This is the kind of stress that is associated with foreboding feelings that the demand or danger is too much, that you are not in control, and that the experience is overwhelming.

The way we perceive a situation determines, to a large extent, if we feel challenge or threat stress, and our perceptions are influenced by our personality traits, temperament, and past experiences. If our perceptions are accurate and realistic, then we are able to mobilize appropriate coping strategies. The problem is that when our perceptions are unrealistic or distorted then our coping responses may not be helpful or appropriate. It is often our unrealistic perceptions that cause us to feel undue threat stress.

For example, our minds are wired to see threat in the environment as a way to maximize our safety and survival. While this can be helpful in avoiding danger, it can cause us to overestimate and exaggerate how bad or stressful things will be and underestimate our ability to cope with stressors. As a result, we all have a tendency to catastrophize, that is to view things as being more awful or unmanageable than they really are.

Back to the example of speaking in front of a group, a person might think, "I will probably make a mistake and people will think that I am stupid" or "They will see my anxiety and view me as weak or immature." This kind of thinking would certainly raise an individual's sense of threat and level of stress and anxiety. If, on the other hand, a person thinks, "I might make a mistake, but it is no big deal, people do it all the time in public speaking," or "I will probably have some anxiety, but most people do when they speak in front of a group, and they will understand." This process would likely result in a person feeling the challenge of giving the presentation but not cause them to feel the level of threat that would make the situation overwhelming.

To deal with our catastrophizing tendencies, it is helpful to write down your worries, stresses and fears then ask yourself the following questions:

- How likely is this to happen?
- If it does happen, how bad can it be?
- How would I cope with it if it happened?
- How will things seem a week from now? A year? Five years?
- Is this really going to affect my future or ruin my life?

Another thinking pattern that contributes to threat stress involves unrealistic expectations or demands we put on ourselves that are usually expressed in the form of "must," "should," and "have to" statements. "I should be handling this better," "I should be more organized," "I should be more spiritual," and many other "shoulds" intrude themselves into our thinking each day. A parent, for example, might think, "I should spend time with my kids, work on my calling and help out at the school this morning." Another person, just out of college might believe, "I just have to get this job if I want to progress in my career."

This type of thinking can be modified by relaxing expectations and turning "shoulds" and "musts" into "preferences" or "likes." In the above examples, it would be less stressful to think, "I would prefer to spend time with my kids, work on my calling, and help out at the school if I have time to do it," or "It would be nice to get this job, but it isn't going to ruin my career if I don't."

Stressful events can also be manageable challenges when we reflect on our past successes with facing difficult situations. Perhaps you survived a serious illness, dealt with a difficult divorce, made it through the death of a family member or close friend, and bounced back from losing a job. These experiences can give you confidence that you have the ability to cope with current stressful events, even if you don't always do it in a stellar manner.

Keeping on Top of Time

For many of us, managing our time effectively is a challenging task and is one of the most common cause of stress. Statement such as, "where did all my time go?" "I never have enough time to get things done," and "I wasn't able to get anything productive accomplished today" are typical time mismanagement issues.

Keeping control of time usually comes down to a few basic tasks. First, you need to have a way to keep track of your schedule. This might be something as simple as a day planner or a calendar where you can write down appointments and activities. It usually works best to keep appointments in only one planner, phone, or tablet, as opposed to multiple calendars because it is too easy to forget you put an appointment in another device or book and the expected synchronization of calendars from one device to another sometimes does not transpire.

A "to do" list of whatever sort or style is usually indispensable for getting things done because it keeps the tasks of the day in front of you and you can keep track of what has been accomplished, and what has not been. It is easy keep such a list on an electronic device, but for the less technologically savvy individual, an old-fashioned grocery-style list on a piece of paper that you carry in your back pocket or purse can do the job quite effectively.

The next element in managing time is prioritizing tasks. This means deciding which tasks are most important and which ones need to be accomplished first. Most of us have had the experience at the end of the day of realizing that most of our time was spent engaged in things that really were not the top priority. Some of these events may have seemed important or even urgent at the time, but ultimately there were other things more deserving of our time and attention. Take, for example, the common refrain of individuals who feel that they just spent the entire day "putting out fires" or "spinning their wheels." To be sure, some fires have to be extinguished, but in many cases, a clearer view of priorities would have made a significant difference.

There are many ways to prioritize tasks, from the simple to the elaborate. For example, going back to the grocery list mentioned above, assign a priority to each task as it was being written down, or to order the tasks based on priority or preference. Author and consultant Dr. Stephen Covey recommended prioritizing tasks by assigning them to one of four categories:

1. ***Important tasks with urgent deadlines or consequences.*** This would include important work, church or family projects or activities.
2. ***Tasks that are important, but have no deadlines.*** Examples would be exercise, hobbies or planning activities.
3. ***Tasks of daily living.*** Paying bills, organizing papers and cleaning fall into this category.
4. ***Activities of little importance.*** These would include such things as surfing the Internet, playing video games, and watching TV.[2]

Managing distractions is also important because it helps you stay focused on important tasks and activities. There are many kinds of distractions to contend with each day such as social media notifications, emails, texts, and talkative colleagues and co-workers. One strategy to deal with electronic intrusions is to have set times and intervals for checking email, notifications, and returning calls. Instead of responding every time you experience a ding, chime, or vibration, you check and respond to messages at intervals you determine, such as once every hour. Putting your phone away, clearing off magazines and newspapers from your desk, and shutting your door can also help to minimize distractions.

Finally, time blocking is a useful strategy that involves setting a specific amount or block of time to engage in a particular task. This creates a protected space to focus on specific tasks and helps you avoid multitasking, which is usually counterproductive. It also gives you a time frame for completing a task which can sometimes help you stay focused and motivated. You might set longer blocks of time for bigger projects, such as writing, in depth discussions, planning an activity or personal study. Smaller blocks of time can be used for minor tasks like writing emails, returning phone calls, and checking text and social media messages.

Whatever system is used, the main issue is working your plan consistently and taking the time to think about what you want to accomplish and then structure your approach based on priorities. There is no doubt that if you do not tackle tasks in order of importance, then circumstances will often dictate that your time will be filled with tasks and activities that are less important.

Aligning Time and Values

In addition to managing time and prioritizing tasks, how you allocate your time has a significant impact on your stress level. The goal is to align your time allocation with those things that you value most in life so that you can spend most of your time engaged in things that are most important to you. In determining what is most important, ask yourself the following questions: What creates meaning and fulfillment for me? What am I passionate about? What relationships really matter to me?

The answers to these questions might include things such as family relationships, spirituality, service to others, connecting with nature, health, and friendships. If this is indeed the case, then the next step would be to evaluate how well your actual use of time fits with these values. For example, if family relationships are important, you might ask yourself how much time you are spending with your spouse and your children relative to other involvements. Or, if spirituality is a meaningful part of your life, then you could ask how much time you are spending studying scriptures, praying, and serving others.

An easy help for keeping track of how you spend your time is to keep a time log where you take five minutes or less at the end of each day and write down what you did and the amount of time involved. This might be challenging or annoying initially, but if you are persistent, it will quickly become a habit that will yield valuable information about what is happening to your time allotment each day.

The bottom line is that the more time you spend doing things that are out of sync with your goals and values, the more unsettled and stressed you will be. Conversely, the more your time is focused on those things that you value and are passionate about, the greater will be your sense of peace and contentment.

Solving Problems

All of us face problems in our daily lives, ranging from irritations and hassles, such as annoying neighbors or getting into a fender bender on the way to work, to major challenges, such as job loss or the death of a family member. How we approach and attempt to solve these problems plays a major part in determining how stressful the problem is to us.

It is useful in dealing with problems to first consider which problems are changeable and which are not. Relationship difficulties, overscheduling, workloads, and daily routines are changeable problems, while illnesses, death, other people's behavior and some work expectations are not. Problems that are changeable can be approached through a problem solving strategy while those that are not may have to be dealt with through other means, such as modifying expectations, garnering social support, implementing relaxation strategies, and other coping techniques.

Understanding your approach to problems is also a helpful prerequisite to effective problem solving. There are two primary orientations to dealing with problems. The first is the optimistic/realistic style. Those who operate from this framework view problems, however irritating, as a normal part of life and see them as challenges and opportunities to improve. They are also confident that they will be able to overcome their problems with time, effort, and persistence and are able to use a problem solving strategy to manage their challenges

On the other hand, those who operate from the pessimistic/unrealistic perspective feel that problems should not be happening and that many of their problems are unfair. They also view problems as threatening, overwhelming, and requiring too much effort to solve.

Consequently, they try to deal with them through avoidance, blaming, and relying on others for solutions.

To effectively solve problems, you need some kind of problem-solving strategy. Many smaller problems can be solved without reliance on a formal strategy because the solutions are not difficult to see and are fairly straightforward. However, other problems are not so easily handled because they are large and complex or the problem itself is not well understood or defined. In these cases a problem solving strategy can be helpful.

While there are many kinds of problem solving strategies, most have commonalties that can be broken down into five steps:

1. Recognize the problem
2. Clarifying the problem to solve
3. Generating solutions
4. Choosing a solution
5. Developing a plan to implement the solution

It might seem like a simple task to recognize a problem to be solved, and in many instances this is the case. On the other hand, each of us experiences problems from time to time that are not so easy to identify. You can probably think of a time when something was bothering you, but you were not sure exactly what it was. Perhaps the only way you knew something was wrong was because of certain indicators that you had come to recognize as markers of distress for you.

Once a problem has been recognized, the next step is to clarify the specific elements of the problem and how they affect you. Asking yourself questions such as "When do I notice the problem?" "How often does it occur?" "Where does it occur?" "Who is involved?" "How do I feel and what do I do when it happens?" can all be helpful when trying to understand and clarify the problem.

Once you have clarified the problem, you are now in a position to start generating solutions. This process involves a period of brainstorming where you think of a number of possible solutions without censoring or making quick judgments about which is best. All options and possibilities are welcome and all are written down for consideration. Some solutions may seem unrealistic or "far-fetched," but they are still welcome additions to the list of possibilities. You can even ask trusted friends or relatives for their ideas. A review of all proposed solutions can then be undertaken with a systematic "weeding out" of those that appear unworkable or ineffective. Eventually, the solutions that appear to be the most feasible with the best chance of solving the problem is chosen.

Once the solution is chosen, a plan to implement it is constructed with specific details as to how to proceed. This entails the "who, what, when, where, and why" of the plan. Constructing a plan is important because it helps you can break down the implementation into manageable steps and may also reveal potential obstacles that require specific strategies to overcome.

Once the plan is implemented, a review of how you felt about the effectiveness of your solution is undertaken, and ideas as to how to improve it are considered. It is important to remember that your plan of action is not always going to solve the problem. There may have been things you didn't consider when you made your plan, but proved to be important. There are also many factors that contribute to most problems and you may not have been able to impact all of them. Disappointment in the outcome is not unusual and needs to be taken in stride. It is no time for excessive self-criticism or blaming but rather a time to learn from your efforts and to revise your solution.

In today's ever-changing and fast paced world, full of all kinds of demands and changes, learning to manage stress is essential. Effectively accomplishing this is likely to result in better health, improved performance, more satisfying relationships, heightened self-esteem and confidence, and more persistent feelings of calmness and serenity in your life. You will probably also notice a greater desire to serve others, more sensitivity to the spirit, and an increased sense of closeness to the Lord.

Power through the Atonement of Jesus Christ

One final strategy for reducing stress and dealing with all other emotional, spiritual, and physical challenges we face is accessing the power of the Atonement of Jesus Christ. The prophet Alma provided this illuminating description of what Jesus experienced in mortality and, consequently, how He can help us: "And he shall go forth, suffering pains and afflictions and temptations of every kind; and this that the word might be fulfilled which saith he will take upon him the pains and the sicknesses of his people. . . . And he will take upon him their infirmities, that his bowels may be filled with mercy, according to the flesh, that he may know according to the flesh how to succor his people according to their infirmities" (Alma 7:11–12).

President Dallin H. Oaks also taught, "He therefore knows our struggles, our heartaches, our temptations, and our suffering, for He willingly experienced them all as an essential part of His Atonement. . . . Because of His atoning experience in mortality, our Savior is able to comfort, heal, and strengthen all men and women everywhere, but I believe He does so only for those who seek Him and ask for His help."[3]

Certainly, the Lord is aware of our struggles in dealing with stress and other challenges we face, and will provide strength through the Atonement and grace of Jesus Christ. The only requirement is that we ask in faith for His help.

In today's ever changing and fast paced world, full of all kinds of demands and changes, learning to manage stress is essential. Effectively accomplishing this is likely to result in better health, improved performance, more satisfying relationships, heightened self-esteem and confidence, and more persistent feelings of calmness, peace, and serenity in your life. You will probably also notice a greater desire to serve others, more receptivity to the spirit, and an increased sense of closeness to the Lord.

References to Chapter 9

1   Robert Elliot, in *Don't Sweat the Small Stuff* (Hachette, 1997).

2   Stephen R. Covey, *The 7 Habits of Highly Effective People* (New York: Simon & Schuster, 1989).

3   Dallin H. Oaks, "Strengthened by the Atonement of Jesus Christ," *Ensign*, November 2015.

Chapter 10

LIVING A PEACEFUL LIFESTYLE

Lead a quiet and peaceable life in all godliness and honesty.

—1 Timothy 2:2

IN OUR QUEST to live more peaceful and enjoyable lives, it is easy to think of the solution in grand, broad terms, such as buying a home in the mountains or the beach, or moving to an island in the pacific or a country that is more slow-paced and relaxed. While this might be possible for some, most of us are consigned to living where we are presently and trying to somehow improve our ability to experience calmness and tranquility amidst the grind of daily living. The Book of Mormon provides a key to how this can be accomplished in the writings of Alma who taught, "By small and simple things are great things brought to pass" (Alma 37:6).

This counsel is certainly true when it comes to spiritual matters in our own lives, and in the global work of the Lord. Furthermore, the concept of "small and simple things" is also true in many other aspects of our lives, including managing the anxiety and stress of daily challenges and finding some measure of peace in our existence. There are small and simple practices which, if implemented consistently, can help us reach our desired goal.

Caught Up in "Busyness"

A major challenge we face is the constant pull to become caught up in the motion and frenetic activity that is swirling around us. We live in a fast-paced, competitive world where everything moves quickly. As so many of us know, there are many pressures that begin as soon as your morning alarm rings. Our culture is dominated by constant sources of stimulation, much of it technology based, in the form of cell phones, television, computers, and tablets in which we find a vast array of videos, sound bites, posts, tweets, texts, messages, and pics, all available at our fingertips. We also face an endless array of jobs to do, unrelenting pressures to perform at a high level, classes to take, callings to fulfill, kids to care for, games to see, events to attend, trips to take, people to see and places to be. Did we leave anything out? When our lives become inundated with such activities and concerns, as many of us are, our situation can be summed up as toxic and unbalanced "busyness."

While some of these things are important and essential, many are not. Our task, therefore, is to proactively decide where we focus our attention, time, energy, and efforts, while constantly being mindful of the pull to become even busier. Busyness is a major source of stress and anxiety for many of us that negatively affects our sense of well-being and happiness.

It is interesting to note that as a group, members of The Church of Jesus Christ of Latter-day Saints are known to be hard working and industrious; however, sometimes our busyness may seem compulsive or frantic, leading to comments from observers, such as "A good Mormon is a busy Mormon"[1] and "In Mormon culture . . . action is esteemed over contemplation."[2]

Years ago, when Mark and his family lived in the suburbs of Dallas, he had an interesting experience that taught him a great lesson. A family in their ward invited them over to swim in their backyard pool and have a barbeque. The social event was to begin around 4:00 in the afternoon, and the Ogletrees had many things to do before they could eat and socialize later in the day. Some of their children had games that morning, the garage had to be cleaned, the lawn needed to be mowed, and they even had to take a load of stuff to the dump.

Their Saturday was a frantic frenzy, running from one even to the other—like many of your Saturdays. However, when Mark and his family arrived at the home of their friends, he found the father of the home kicked back and relaxed. This good man was lying on a recliner next to his pool, reading his book. When Mark saw this man in such a relaxed position on a Saturday afternoon, he thought, "Is this how other people live? Do most people just chill out on Saturdays, literally relaxing and reading?" Mark had the thought that maybe his family needed to slow down a little bit, and stop and smell the roses—so to speak. Perhaps we all could find ways to chill out and enjoy life more than we do.

There are many reasons that we live such busy lives, including feelings of anxiety and guilt stemming from the belief that busyness is, in and of itself, a requirement for righteous living and a way to justify our existence. Moreover, slowing down and stopping to focus on the present may be viewed an unnecessary hindrance or distraction.

In contrast, Elder Dieter F. Uchtdorf has said,

> Isn't it true that we often get so busy? And sad to say, we even wear our busyness as a badge of honor, as though being busy, by itself, was an accomplishment or sign of a superior life. Is it? I think of our Lord and exemplar, Jesus Christ, and his short life among the people of Galilee and Jerusalem. I have tried to imagine him bustling around between meetings or multitasking to get a list of urgent things accomplished. I can't see it.[3]

Unfortunately, busyness is the new status symbol. No longer do the prizes go to the wealthiest or even the most popular but to the busiest. Elder Joseph B. Wirthlin taught, "Sometimes we feel that the busier we are, the more important we are—as though our busyness defines our worth."[4] He also emphasized, "Being busy is not necessarily being spiritual."[5]

Busyness can also be driven by ambition to accomplish and excel. While seeking success and accomplishments are generally good things, unbridled strivings for status, power, money, and recognition can lead to a compulsive orientation toward task completion and workaholism. For some, filling every minute with activity becomes a way to avoid feelings of meaninglessness, emptiness, and loneliness or an effort to bolster a failing sense of importance. Many other individuals also have bought into the mistaken belief that if they can just stay busy with so many things, then they will *not* have time to worry, fear, or be stressed. However, anxiety always has a way of catching up to us—especially if we do not take care of our spiritual, mental, emotional, and physical health.

Stillness, Presence and Reflection

The antidote to help relieve the tension and turmoil of constant busyness and stimulation is found in Doctrine and Covenants 101:16, where the Lord counsels us to "Be still and know that I am God." In this verse, the Lord charges his Saints to make space in our lives for stillness and calm where we can decompress, settle our minds, and hear his voice. This verse reminds us that God is in control of our lives—not us! Doing this requires us to intentionally slow down, retreat from social media, and put our many tasks on hold for a period of time.

In a devotional address at BYU-Idaho in November 2007, John Thomas reported an experience of President Brigham Young that underscores the need to slow down:

> On a Sunday in August 1845 Brigham Young paused from the demands of leadership to record a dream he'd had the previous night. "I dreamed . . . I saw Brother Joseph Smith," he wrote, "and as I was going about my business, he said, "Brother Brigham, don't be in a hurry." Joseph repeated the counsel twice more, with some "degree of sharpness": "Brother Brigham, don't be in a hurry. Brother Brigham, don't be in a hurry" (History of the Church, 7:435).[6]

The value of disengaging from the turmoil of the world, to experience stillness, or even idleness, was described by Tim Kreider in the *New York Times*:

> Idleness is not just a vacation, an indulgence or a vice; it is as indispensable to the brain as vitamin D is to the body, and

deprived of it we suffer a mental affliction as disfiguring as rickets. The space and quiet that idleness provides is a necessary condition for standing back from life and seeing it whole, for making unexpected connections and waiting for the wild summer lightning strikes of inspiration—it is, paradoxically, necessary to getting any work done. . . . History is full of stories of inspirations that come in idle moments and dreams. It almost makes you wonder whether loafers, goldbricks, and no-accounts aren't responsible for more of the world's great ideas, inventions and masterpieces than the hardworking.[7]

Some of our greatest insights and sparks of inspiration come when we are calm, still, and not consciously working on anything, or when we are engaged in meditation, gospel study, pondering, contemplation, or reflection. President Gordon B. Hinckley was a champion of the importance of taking time to think and meditate. He taught,

I heard President David O. McKay say to the members of the Twelve on one occasion, "Brethren, we do not spend enough time meditating."

I believe that with all my heart. Our lives become extremely busy. We run from one thing to another. We wear ourselves out in thoughtless pursuit of goals which are highly ephemeral. We are entitled to spend some time with ourselves in introspection, in development. I remember my dear father when he was about the age that I am now. He lived in a home where there was a rock wall on the grounds. It was a low wall, and when the weather was warm, he would go and sit on his wall. It seemed to me he sat there for hours, thinking, meditating, pondering things that he would say and write, for he was a very gifted speaker and writer. He read much, even into his very old age. He never ceased growing. Life was for him a great adventure in thinking.[8]

The recent COVID-19 pandemic had a significant impact on our health, economy, and lifestyle. The prolonged "shelter in place" left many without jobs or with significantly reduced hours. Children were not able to go to school, and many individuals spent a significant number of days at home without much personal interaction with the outside world.

While this was a challenging circumstance in many respects, with much suffering, there were positives that resulted from the "forced slowdown." Most notable was that many people had to ratchet down their busy lifestyles because of the necessity of working at home, schooling their children at home, and following the guidelines of social distancing. As a result, families spent more time together, talking, playing, and laughing. We saw things going on in our neighborhoods that did not often happen, such as parents and children playing games together in their driveways, people going for walks and bicycle rides, and neighbors talking to each other (at a safe distance, of course). People also had more time to read, think, and meditate. There was time for self-reflection regarding personal aspirations and goals, time to evaluate progress and challenges, and space to consider possible course corrections.

During the pandemic, Elder Jeffrey R. Holland was interviewed by the *Church News* and made the following comments:

This is a rare time of enforced solitude when we don't have a lot of trivia or superficial busyness distracting us from considering the truly important things in life . . . ," said the member of the Quorum of the Twelve Apostles. "Such times invite us to look into our soul and see if we like what we see there. Let's realize this is one of the times we can take the saddle off our backs, a time when not quite so many demands are made and we can address edifying, eternally important things. When we are engaged in society, a person's mind is often consumed with matters of current affairs and chatty conversation," he said.

"But when we're alone, those are times of character assessment. That's when you think about who you really are and what really matters. . . . It is a sobering exercise to be quiet, to be alone with yourself. The obvious question then is, Do you like the company you are keeping when you are the only one in the room?[9]

During the pandemic, there were opportunities to be more aware of the present moment: the beautiful flowers and trees, the warmth of sunshine, the vastness of the sky, the chirping of birds and movements of animals. In addition, we had enough quiet and freedom to contemplate the grandeur of God and His creations, to consider one's relationship with Him, to feel His love and yearning to be a part of our lives, to "be still and know that I am God."

When asked about the change in lifestyle associated with the "shelter in place," most people we talked to admitted that although they did not like the reason for the changes, they enjoyed the benefits of slowing down and were not looking forward to resuming their fast pace, or their busy and high stress lifestyles. Likewise, in a recent general conference address, President Russell M. Nelson observed:

For a time, the pandemic canceled activities that would normally fill our lives. We may be able to choose to fill time again with the noise and commotion of the world. Or we can use our time to hear the voice of the Lord whispering His guidance, comfort, and peace. Quiet time is sacred time—time that will facilitate personal revelation and instill peace.[10]

Engaging in stillness, solitude, and meditation is rejuvenating to your mind, body, and spirit and opens the door to revelation and renewal. However, like most things it is not easy to do consistently. It is more likely to happen if you can find a time, usually the same time each day, to pull away from the hustle and bustle of life and enjoy quiet, stillness, and calm. It is in these moments that you can feel more connected to God and more open to the still small voice of the spirit that brings inspiration, consolation and comfort as well as peace, joy, and contentment (See Galatians 5:22–23).

Contentment

Contentment is an unsung personal quality that, while not talked about much, can be an important part of developing a peaceful lifestyle. The Apostle Paul taught, "godliness with contentment is great gain" (1 Timothy 6:6), and the prophet Alma observed, "I ought to be content with the things God hath allotted unto me" (Alma 29:3). Contentment can be described as an acceptance and appreciation for what we have, who we are, and the circumstances in which we find ourselves. It is a willingness to find satisfaction in the present—whatever your situation in life may be and whatever you may be currently experiencing.

We live in a world where there is great emphasis on consumer driven materialism—money, cars, and houses—as well as on accomplishments—awards, recognition, promotions, and other accolades. While these attainments bring with them feelings of pleasure and enjoyment, our minds soon become accustomed to what we have received and achieved, and we seek more. This pattern of becoming dissatisfied with seeking pleasure has been termed the *Hedonic Treadmill*. No matter how fast we go in our pursuit of pleasure we always end up in the same place—feeling dissatisfied and looking for more.

Contentment, on the other hand, takes the focus off what we wish we had and how we would like things to be and places it on acceptance of how things are and what we do have. Moreover, there is less focus on how you were or what you want to be and more focus on enjoying the present. For example, a woman may think that life would be so much better when she moves up in her career and can afford to buy a nice house and take long vacations to foreign countries. While there may be some value in these things, an attitude of contentment would involve an appreciation for what she currently does have—her job, the opportunity to take short vacations, and positive relationships with co-workers.

Contentment does not mean complacency or an absence of aspirations and ambitions but an acceptance of current circumstances that does not preclude desires for a better future or interest in self-improvement. Elder Neal A. Maxwell taught, "Hence, we can and 'ought to be content with the things allotted to us,' being circumstantially content but without being self-satisfied and behaviorally content with ourselves."[11]

Contentment also implies an acceptance of difficult circumstances such as physical illnesses and disabilities, mental heath problems, troublesome marriages and family relationships, financial setbacks, and a host of other challenges that come with mortal life. Through our efforts, and with the Lord's help, we may be able to make improvements in some of these challenging situations, although others may be beyond our control or influence. In those cases, contentment may be difficult but possible and result in significant personal growth. To enjoy greater feelings of contentment in your life, we recommend the following:

1. *Focus on what you have in the present* and savor the small and simple pleasures of daily living, such as taking a walk in nature, enjoying a conversation with a friend, eating a nice meal, spending time with a child, and laughing together. Do not be so concerned with what is coming around the next corner—enjoy today!

2. *Practice gratitude.* Although we have discussed gratitude in other chapters of this book, it is worth mentioning here that expressing appreciation to God and others for what you have and to be thankful for what others have done for you puts life in perspective. Learn to focus on what you do have instead of dwelling on what you lack.

3. *Be careful about comparing yourself to others.* It is hard to feel content when you slip into making comparisons. We usually compare our worst qualities and attainments with the best qualities and accomplishments of others and inevitably fall short. Instead, focus on self-acceptance and making self-improvements based on your values and goals.

4. *Stop buying and accumulating to feel better.* Challenge hedonic thinking, such as: "If I only had . . ." or "when I get this . . ." and try to focus on distinguishing between wants and needs, and simplifying your life. Learn to view wealth in terms of experiences and blessings instead of dollars and cents.

5. *Continue working on personal growth and spiritual development while acknowledging current constraints and limitations.* There are things that each of us will not have the opportunity to do or the ability to attain. However, there are still many opportunities for progress, especially as it involves our spiritual growth. Elder Maxwell observed, "Thus, developing greater contentment within certain of our existing constraints and opportunities is one of our challenges . . . within our givens are unused opportunities for service all about

us. . . . Furthermore, varied as our allotted circumstances may be, we can still keep the commandments of God!"[12]

Embracing Change

Change is an inevitable part of life and is always occurring. Our response to change is also inevitable and can lead to frustration and suffering or can be a catalyst for growth and resilience. Things rarely stay the same in our lives. Our society is fast paced and mobile as evidenced by the frequency with which people change jobs, move to new locations, change wards, and change friends. Some changes are more subtle and silent, such as growing old.

Much of our anxiety and angst is related to our anticipation of change since we usually do not like it. It is not unusual for a young child to complain about having to give up a pacifier or being required to go to school. Adults complain about getting old and having to deal with kids growing up and leaving home. Other adults complain about their adult children coming back home to roost for a season while they figure out their lives.

Change is hard for most of us because we like routine and predictability and we dislike the unknown. Sometimes people stay in bad situations, such as abusive relationships, because it is at least something that is familiar and known. In fact, some prefer being in an abusive relationship because at least they "have someone" in their life. Fears that things might not be as good as they are now and concerns about failing, feeling overwhelmed or unhappy, or not being able to cope underscore many of the anxieties about change.

Much of our resistance to change is due to the fear of loss. Change, in all of its forms, inevitably carries with it the uncomfortable and sometimes painful experience of loss. A move to a new city is associated with the loss of friends and associates in the previous community, a loss of familiar landmarks and a familiar living environment. Growing older is connected with bodily changes, such as losing hair and acquiring wrinkles, along with less stamina and diminished mental acuity. A sense of loss can also be experienced when leaving a comfortable home or having to part with a valued pet.

Ted recalls an experience of loss that involved a car:

Just prior to getting married, I bought a sportscar that I loved driving. About ten years into our marriage, when we had three young children, it became apparent that the sports car was not practical or functional for our family. With a fair amount of dismay, I put the car up for sale. Not surprisingly, it did not take long for the car to sell. Before I knew it, the buyer was driving away from our house in "my" sportscar. Our five-year-old son, who loved the car too, stood with me on the porch and we paid our last respects to our once prized possession. When the car was just about out of sight, my son turned to me with tears in his eyes and emphatically stated, "Mom thinks this is a good idea, but I'm really sad about it." And so was I! Loss is difficult!

As we grapple with processing the changes that occur in our lives, remember that it is our resistance to change that causes most of our suffering, not the changes themselves. Our task is to replace resistance to change with embracing change. We need to work on accepting that change is inevitable and a significant part of life, and embracing change is much less painful than resisting it. Some of the realities that are worth embracing include:

- "you are going to age"
- "you are going to have to leave home"
- "your kids are going to grow up"
- "friendships change over time"
- "friends and family sometimes move away"
- "people get sick, have accidents, and sometimes die"

Another helpful perspective about change is that it might actually lead to improvement. In fact, there are bright spots in most changes that need to be discovered. Ted recalls, "When our last child left home, my wife and I experienced some sadness and loss. We soon discovered, however, that there were some positives about this change, including the opportunity to spend more time together, more flexibility with our time, and more opportunities to serve."

Life changes can also lead to the development of new relationships. Moving to a new community, relocating to a new ward or stake, starting a new job, attending college, serving a mission, and joining a civic organization all offer the prospect of meeting new people and developing relationships, some of which might turn into lasting friendships.

Change can also be a catalyst for significant personal growth. Sometimes it takes a significant change in our lives to create opportunities that lead to expanded capacities and skills. Moving to a new school, changing jobs, taking care of a sick spouse or family member, and receiving a challenging church calling might all result in stretching that ultimately makes us more capable and mature. Children who leave home to attend college or serve missions often report major leaps in confidence and skill in dealing with the world as a result of their challenge to function more independently.

The life changes we experience often lead to new roles and responsibilities that need to be understood and embraced. For example, as their children grow older and move into the teen years and beyond, parents gradually shift from being directors and decision makers in their children's lives to being collaborators, consultants and supporters. In the work environment, as you become more senior, you might move into the role of mentor and consultant instead of manager or boss. This is also true in families where grandparents take a mentoring role and focus on passing on knowledge, family narratives, and specific kinds of skills to their posterity.

As we learn to embrace change instead of resisting it, we open ourselves up to new experiences and increase our capacity for growth and improvement. Moreover, anxiety about the future will be replaced by greater personal resilience, confidence and inner peace.

Taking Care of Your Body

Taking care of our physical bodies is an important but often overlooked aspect of our daily living. However, taking care of our physical selves has a significant impact on our spirituality and our ability to feel good and enjoy life. The importance of taking care of our bodies was recently emphasized by President Russell M. Nelson who said:

> I stand in awe of the miracle of the human body. It is a magnificent creation, essential to our gradual ascent toward

our ultimate divine potential. We cannot progress without it. In giving us the gift of a body, God has allowed us to take a vital step toward becoming more like Him. . . . Your body is your personal temple, created to house your eternal spirit. Your care of that temple is important.[13]

Three important aspects of taking care of our bodies are exercise, sleep and nutrition. In discussing factors that contribute to receiving revelation for our personal lives, Elder Richard G. Scott counseled, "Spiritual communication can be enhanced by good health practices. Exercise, reasonable amounts of sleep, and good eating habits increase our capacity to receive and understand revelation. We will live for our appointed life span. However, we can improve both the quality of our service and our well-being by making careful, appropriate choices."[14]

In addition to contributing to our ability to receive spiritual communication, exercise has multiple positive effects on physical and mental health, including better cardiovascular and immune functioning, decreased anxiety and depression, lower stress levels, better sleep, improved cognitive efficiency, and increased self-esteem. Recent studies have also revealed that people who exercise perceive fewer problems in their lives, and the more physically active we are, the less biological aging takes place in our bodies.[15] In addition to the intrinsic enjoyments of exercise, we have found that exercise routines (mostly running and biking) to be times for effective problem solving, self-reflection, and receiving spiritual impressions.

The biggest challenge with exercise is finding a type of exercise you like or can at least tolerate, making time to do it consistently, and not trying to do too much too fast. There are ways of improving the likelihood that you will have a positive experience with exercising and improve your chances of continuing a consistent pattern; including involving a friend in your routine; starting off easy so you can experience some success; and listening to music, reading, or watching TV while you exercise.

Getting adequate sleep is also essential to health and vitality. Unfortunately, we are a nation of sleep deprived individuals. In a study by the American Psychological Association, 42 percent of adults reported lying awake at night because of stress.[16] Not getting adequate sleep is detrimental to our health and day-to-day functioning. Sleep deprivation is associated with increased stress, irritability, anxiety, and depression. It also interferes with concentration and memory, lowers energy levels, and increases the risk of inflammation and Alzheimer's disease. There are many things that interfere with sleeping well, including stress, anxiety, work, television, social media, and hobbies.

There are some quick tests you can complete that will give you an idea of whether you are getting enough sleep at night. First, if you find yourself falling asleep during the day at work, school, or anytime you are sitting down and unoccupied during the day, then you are probably not sleeping enough at night. Also, if you have to wake up with an alarm or need a power nap during the day, you may not be getting enough sleep. In each case, try going to bed fifteen minutes earlier. If nothing changes, retire another fifteen minutes earlier and so on until you are sleeping enough. Getting on a sleeping schedule, relaxing before going to bed, avoiding things that are stimulating before bed (television, texting, work projects, planning activities), can all be helpful. If your sleep problems do not improve with practicing good sleep hygiene or if they become worse, you should probably consult a medical professional who specializes in sleep problems.

As a nation, our eating habits are not much better than our ability to sleep well. We suffer from unhealthy eating styles and choices which affects our health and well-being. Our western diet is loaded with fats, sugar, and refined carbs, which has led to an obesity epidemic among our children and a myriad physical ailments in adults, including diabetes, heart disease, and an increased risk for various types of cancers.

A few relatively minor changes to our traditional western diet can make a significant difference in our well-being. Cutting back on sweets and sodas; minimizing intake of foods high in fat; reducing sodium; and adding more fruits, vegetables, and whole grains would be a good start. Eating healthier snacks, such as fruits, nuts, yogurt, and vegetables can also be helpful.[17]

Dealing with cravings for snacks between meals can be a formidable challenge. One way to determine whether you are actually hungry or craving food for other reasons, such as reducing stress or boredom, is the apple test. When you feel the need to eat something, try reaching for an apple first. If that is appealing, then you are probably hungry, if not, you may be craving food for other reasons, and it is probably time to think about what might be motivating you to eat.

Making small and simple changes in various aspects of your day-to-day living that you are able to do consistently can lead to noticeable and welcomed changes in your ability to experience more peaceful living. Slowing down, becoming more content, accepting change and taking care of your body are all helpful things, but are likely to be challenging to embrace and integrate.

We recommend starting small and simple, perhaps picking one thing to work on (or part of one thing) and making it easy enough so that you can experience some success. For example, if you have a problem getting enough sleep then start with going to bed fifteen minutes earlier each night for one week, and assess your progress before moving on. Counseling with the Lord and seeking His help regarding what changes to make and how to make them can bring hope and power to the process.

References to Chapter 10

1   Kenneth Woodward, "The Presidency's Mormon Moment," *New York Times*, April 9, 2007.

2   Philip L. Barlow, "Toward a Mormon Sense of Time," *Journal of Mormon History*, 33, no. 1, 2007, 11.

3   Dieter F. Uchtdorf, "Of Regrets and Resolutions," *Ensign,* November 2012.

4   Joseph B. Wirthlin, "Follow Me," *Ensign*, May 2002.

5   Joseph B. Wirthlin, "The Unspeakable Gift," *Ensign*, May 2003.

6   John Thomas, "Don't Be in a Hurry," BYU-Idaho Devotional, November 6, 2007, https://www.byui.edu/devotionals/brother-john-c-thomas.

7   Tim Kreider, "The Busy Trap," *New York Times*, June 30, 2012.

8   Gordon B. Hinckley, Life's Obligations," *Ensign*, February 1999.

9   "'Shelter in place' spiritually and physically, Elder Holland says as isolation orders continue around the world," *Church News,* April 1, 2020.

10   Russell M. Nelson, "What We Are Learning and Will Never Forget," *Ensign,* May 2021.

11   Neal A. Maxwell, "Content with the Things Allotted unto Us," *Ensign*, May 2000.

12   Maxwell.

13   Russell M. Nelson, "We Can Do Better and Be Better," *Ensign,* May 2019.

14   Richard G. Scott, "How to Receive Revelation and Inspiration for Your Personal Life," *Ensign,* May 2012.

15   See Larry Tucker, "Move More, Stress Less," *Ensign*, August 2004; also "High levels of exercise linked to nine years of less aging at the cellular level," *Science Daily*, May 10, 2017.

16   American Psychological Association, "Stress in America," February 4, 2015, https://www.apa.org/news/press/releases/stress/2014/stress-report.pdf.

17   See Michael Greger, *How Not To Die* (New York: Flatiron Books, 2015), 6–10.

Chapter 11

ALLEVIATING ANXIETY AND STRESS WITH GRATITUDE

Are you ever burdened with a load of care?
Does the cross seem heavy you are called to bear?
Count your many blessings; ev'ry doubt will fly
And you will be singing as the days go by.

—"Count Your Blessings," *Hymns*, no. 241

WE ARE AWARE of a father who shared the following experience. He was quite athletic, and during his adolescence and early adulthood, he often thought how exciting it would be to one day marry and have children. Because of his background in sports, he fantasized of perhaps having five or six sons that he would coach in Little League baseball, basketball, and Pop Warner football. He even thought of how exciting it would be, as his boys became adults, to play on the same softball team together. He also dreamed of other outdoor recreation with his future children, such as hunting, fishing, and skiing.

This man ultimately married and, along with his wife, started their family. Their first baby was a girl—something he never even considered. In fact, as each baby came, each one was a girl! Over a period of several years, this man became the proud father of five daughters. Please do not misunderstand—this man loved his daughters. In fact, he learned that he could play sports with several of them. Two of them ultimately became college athletes. Even though he was happy and fulfilled, he still longed to have a son, but it never happened. Finally, he and his wife gave up on that idea, and focused on raising their beautiful, wonderful daughters.

As his girls became teenagers, this father visited a doctor for a routine physical exam. Because of a problem that was detected, he was referred to a urologist for further testing. After a complete exam, the doctor detected a significant issue with the man's reproductive system. The urologist said to the man, "Do you have any children?" The man replied, "Yes, we have five beautiful daughters." The doctor exclaimed, "That's impossible. Men with your condition usually are infertile." As the man left the doctor's office that day, his heart swelled with gratitude. No longer would he whine or complain that he did not have enough sons to field a softball team. He was simply grateful that he and his wife were able to conceive a child, let alone, multiple children. After that day in the doctor's office, this man's prayers were often filled with gratitude for his five daughters.

Similarly, years ago, renowned writer Stephen King was the victim of a serious car accident. He was walking on a country road when a distracted driver plowed into him with a van. King was hospitalized with multiple fractures to his right leg and hip. He also had a collapsed lung, broken ribs, and a severe scalp laceration. Later, King was asked what he was thinking when he was told by the medical staff that probably should have died. After all, not many people survive being hit by a van going at highway speed. King replied with one powerful word: "Gratitude."[1] Indeed, King could have focused on all of his injuries, setbacks, hours of physical therapy, and recovery, or he could simply be grateful that he was alive.

Gratitude is a powerful Christlike attribute that seems to have a similar significance and potency as other Christlike attributes such as faith, hope, charity, and meekness. Roman orator Cicero taught that gratitude was "not only the greatest of virtues, but the parent of all the others."[2] Melody Beatty, the author of almost twenty self-help books, including *Codependent No More*, once explained, "Gratitude unlocks the fullness of life. It turns what we have into enough, and more. It turns denial into acceptance, chaos into order, confusion into clarity. It can turn a meal into a feast, a house into a home, a stranger into a friend. . . . Gratitude makes sense of our past, brings peace for today, and creates vision for tomorrow."[3]

According to the Latter-day Saint Gospel Topics library, "Gratitude is a feeling of appreciation and thankfulness for blessings or benefits we have received. As we cultivate a grateful attitude, we are more likely to be happy and spiritually strong. . . . Gratitude is an uplifting, exalting attitude. People are generally happier when they have gratitude in their hearts. We cannot be bitter, resentful, or mean-spirited when we are grateful."[4] The expression of gratitude has the ability to help us enjoy life, to be content, and to have a healthy perspective of both good and bad experiences. Moreover, gratitude connects us on a deeper level with our Father in Heaven, and helps us recognize His hand in our lives.

Too many of us do not think of gratitude or practice it enough. Although many individuals and families consider being grateful around Thanksgiving each year, that is not enough time to consider our enormous blessings and to live in a constant spirit of thankfulness. One research study reported that those who are religious express gratitude more than those who are nonreligious. In fact, 75 percent of the religious respondents in the study agreed with the statement, "I have so much in life to be thankful for," compared to 39 percent of the nonreligious. Not surprising, this study also reported that the younger people are, the less likely they are to express gratitude. In the same study, only 35 percent of 18–24 year olds reported that they expressed gratitude often, compared with 57 percent of those 65 or older. Overall, only 52 percent of women and 44 percent of men express gratitude on a regular basis.[5]

When it comes to expressing gratitude, most of can do better. Indeed, we should "count our many blessings" daily, not just at the end of November each year. Hence, gratitude should not be dictated by seasons, but by how we choose to live each day. To live a joyous life, we should become keenly aware of what we *do* have instead of focusing on what we *lack*. Dr. Robert Emmons, a psychologist who has spent most of his professional life studying the benefits of gratitude, has written "Being grateful is an acknowledgment that there are good and enjoyable things in the world."[6] He also explained, "Gratefulness is a knowing awareness that we are the recipients of goodness."[7]

To be grateful for our blessings, we must be aware of what God has given us. However, once we are aware, we should express our thanks to those who have blessed us—especially to our Father in Heaven. In fact, to be ungrateful is offensive to our God. The Savior taught, "And in nothing doth man offend God, or against none is his wrath kindled, save those who confess not his hand in all things, and obey not his commandments" (Doctrine and Covenants 59:21). We are also taught in the scriptures that we should give thanks for everything (Doctrine and Covenants 98:1; see also 1 Thessalonians 5:18). As we express gratitude to our Heavenly Father often, we will experience peace, contentment, and joy in our lives. We will be able to put our problems in perspective, and rejoice in the simplicities of life.

The Doctrine of Gratitude

The scriptures and teachings of our apostles and prophets are brimming with principles regarding gratitude. For instance, in the Book of Mormon we are taught to arise daily with hearts "full of thanks unto God" (Alma 37:37). In addition, in the Book of Alma, we learn that we should "live in thanksgiving daily" (Alma 34:38). That is right—we should celebrate Thanksgiving each day—not just occasionally or seasonally. Can you imagine how wonderful our lives would be if we were focused on our blessings instead of our trials, our struggles, and our disappointments? President Joseph F. Smith declared, "The grateful man sees so much in the world to be thankful for, and with him the good outweighs the evil. Love overpowers jealousy, and light drives darkness out of his life. Pride destroys our gratitude and sets up selfishness in its place. How much happier we are in the presence of a grateful and loving soul, and how careful we should be to cultivate, through the medium of a prayerful life, a thankful attitude toward God and man!"[8]

Gratitude is a saving principle of the gospel. Without sincere thankfulness, it would be difficult to obtain all that our Father in Heaven has in store for us. The Prophet Joseph Smith taught, "If you will thank the Lord with all of your heart, every night, for all the blessings of that day, you will eventually find yourself exalted in the kingdom of God."[9] Likewise, our Savior taught, "he who receives all things with thankfulness shall be made glorious" (Doctrine and Covenants 78:19). Elder James E. Talmage further explained, "Gratitude is an ennobling quality in man; and he in whose soul it has not place is [defective]. Gratitude is twin sister to humility; pride is a foe to both. The man who has come into close communion with God cannot fail to be thankful; for he feels, he knows, that for all he has and all he is, he is indebted to the Supreme Giver."[10]

President Gordon B. Hinckley addressed those who do not express gratitude when he stated, "Absence of gratitude is the mark of the narrow, uneducated mind. It bespeaks a lack of knowledge and the ignorance of self-sufficiency. It expresses itself in ugly egotism and frequently wanton mischief. . . . Where there is appreciation, there is courtesy, there is concern for the rights and property of others. Without it, there is arrogance and evil."[11]

There is a strong connection between happiness and gratitude. Gratitude is the key to a happy, optimistic, and joyful life. If you are feeling anxious, stressed, sad, depressed, or blue, begin to count your blessings, and happiness will return. Elder Joseph B. Wirthlin summarized, "I believe that many people are unhappy because they have not learned to be grateful."[12] Another author wrote, "All happy people are grateful, and ungrateful people cannot be happy. . . . Because gratitude is the key to happiness, anything that undermines gratitude must undermine happiness."[13] David Steindl-Rast, a Benedictine monk, wrote, "The root of joy is gratefulness. . . . It is not joy that makes us grateful; it is gratitude that makes us joyful."[14] Gratitude and happiness are deeply connected. If you want to have a happier life, learn to be grateful, and express your gratitude often. If you want to live a life with less stress, and less depression, and less anxiety, focus on gratitude.

Furthermore, gratitude allows us to change our focus from all that is wrong in the world, to that which is right, happy, healthy, joyful, positive, and uplifting. For instance, gratitude can help an individual change their focus from being financially poor to focusing on the good things they have in their life, like their faith, their family, and their hopes and dreams. Gratitude helps us focus on what we have instead of what we do not have or what we have lost. Indeed, we could complain for hours and days about our terrible car, and how embarrassing it is to drive, or we could be grateful that at least we have a means to get ourselves around town.

Consider President Russell M. Nelson, our Prophet and President of the Church of Jesus Christ of Latter-day Saints. In a message called, "The Healing Power of Gratitude," he recounted the death of his wife Dantzel, and the loss of two of his daughters to cancer. He then stated,

> No parent is prepared to lose a child. And yet, despite these and other difficult experiences, I am incredibly, eternally grateful for so very many things. I am grateful to God for the nearly 60 years Dantzel and I shared together, for a lifetime of love and joy and cherished memories. And I thank Him for my wife, Wendy, who I met after Dantzel's passing. She now fills my life with joy. I am grateful to God for the years I had with my two departed daughters. This father's heart melts when I see attributes of those girls in the precious faces of their children and grandchildren.[15]

We admire President Russell M. Nelson and his counsel on gratitude. Instead of focusing on losing his wife and two of his daughters to death, he has chosen to focus on the wonderful, incredible times that they actually had together. He treasures his memories with Dantzel, Emily, and Wendy. Think of the joy that such a concept can bring into all of our lives!

Nevertheless, some individuals choose, instead, to focus on all of their problems: losses, reverses, tragedy, heartbreak, bankruptcy, cancer, war, terror, elections, and the economy. However, a hyper-focus on these things will not do us much good—most of these things are completely out of our control anyway. What we do have control over is how we choose to think about our circumstances. Why not focus on the good in the world—our blessings, our families, our testimonies, living prophets, the Atonement, and the plan of salvation? Consider that most of us woke up this morning and took a hot shower, followed by a nice breakfast. Many of us then drove a decent car to work. Today, most of us will not have to swim across shark-infested waters to get home; we will most likely engage in some form of entertainment, eat some good food, and fall asleep in a warm bed. Not everyone in the world will enjoy such privileges that so many of us take for granted. We have so many bounteous blessings. If you do not believe that, visit a third-world country for a day and you will most likely change your mind.

The Benefits of Gratitude

Dr. Robert Emmons stated, "Gratitude is literally one of the few things that can measurably change people's lives."[16] Although there are literally hundreds of psychological benefits to practicing gratitude, consider the following:

- Practicing gratitude can lead to increases in optimism, vitality, happiness, a sense of well-being, and greater satisfaction with life.[17]
- Gratitude is related to individuals who are generous and compassionate towards others.[18]
- Grateful people also report feeling less envious and more generous with their possessions. Moreover, they enjoy better quality relationships.[19]
- Those who are grateful report more resistance to stress, adversity, serious trauma, and suffering.[20]
- Regarding mental health, those who express gratitude reported less stress, envy, resentment, regret, depression, and hopelessness.[21]
- Social benefits to gratitude include stronger relationships, greater quality in relationships, deeper emotional connections to others, more willing to forgive others, and stronger, more positive relationships with children and other family members.[22]
- From a physiological standpoint, gratitude has been related to improved immune system functioning, lower blood pressure, better kidney health, lower levels of stress hormones, lower levels of heart disease, increased sleep quality, and longer sleep duration.[23]
- In one study, people who regularly kept a gratitude journal and often verbally expressed their gratitude reported feeling closer and more connected to people, had better relationships, were more likely to help others, felt less lonely, felt less depressed,

slept better, and were more pleasant to be around.[24]

Dr. Robert Emmons has spent most of his professional life study-ing positive psychology and gratitude. In one investigation, Dr. Emmons conducted a ten-week gratitude study. His team of research-ers placed participants in three groups. One group was encouraged to briefly record five things they were grateful for each week. A second group was asked to describe five hassles or negative events that had happened to them each week. Then the third group was invited to list five events, but they were not told to categorize them as positive or negative.

Prior to each participant writing about their blessings or their hassles, they completed a daily journal where they rated their moods, their physical health, and their overall well-being. Mood rating included feelings such as distress, excitement, sadness, stress, and hap-piness. They also rated their physical health, noting symptoms such as headaches, sore muscles, stomach pain, nausea, coughing, sore throat, and poor appetite. Finally, the participants rated how they felt about their lives, selecting descriptions that varied between delighted to terrible. The results of the ten-week study were fascinating. Dr. Ray Huntington explained,

> The gratitude participants felt better about their lives and were more optimistic about the future than people in the other two groups. The gratitude group also reported fewer health concerns, like headaches, and spent significantly more time exercising than people in the other two groups. According to the scale Dr. Emmons used to calculate well-being, the people in the gratitude group were a full 25 percent happier than the participants in the hassles or neutral groups.[25]

Without question, the expression of gratitude can have a power-ful, positive impact on our mental, emotional, and physical health. The more we live in a state of daily thanksgiving, the happier we will be, and the better we will feel. Our stress and anxiety will decrease, and we will be in a better position to help those around us be kinder and happier.

Gratitude and Anxiety

Gratitude is a powerful antidote to anxiety, fear, and worry. Just as doubt and fear cannot exist in the same mind at the same time, nether can gratitude and anxiety exist in the same mind at the same time! If we are focused on our blessings and God's goodness, it is difficult to be full of stress, fear, and worry. President Thomas S. Monson explained, "We can lift ourselves, and others as well, when we refuse to remain in the realm of negative thought and cultivate within our hearts an attitude of gratitude."[26] Elder Robert D. Hales added that gratitude could cleanse us, heal us, and bring peace into our lives "that helps us overcome the pain of adversity and failure."[27]

Expressing gratitude helps us to focus on the blessings in our lives and discount the trouble that may surround us. Being grateful helps to strip ourselves of selfishness and puts our problems in perspective. Christian author Max Lucado explained,

> Gratitude is a mindful awareness of the benefits of life. It is the greatest of virtues. Studies have linked the emotion with a variety of positive effects. Grateful people tend to be more empathetic and forgiving of others. People who keep a gratitude journal are more likely to have a positive outlook on life. Grateful individuals demonstrate less envy, materialism, and self-centeredness. Gratitude improves self-esteem and enhances relationships, quality of sleep, and longevity. If it came in pill form, gratitude would be deemed the miracle cure. It's no wonder, then, that God's anxiety therapy includes a large, delightful dollop of gratitude.[28]

Lucado then explained the relationship between gratitude, stress, and anxiety when he stated,

> As you look at your blessings, take note of what happens. Anxiety grabs his bags and slips out the back door. Worry refuses to share the heart with gratitude. One heartfelt thank-you will suck the oxygen out of worry's world. So say it often. Focus more on what you do have and less on what you don't.[29]

There are great mental health benefits to practicing gratitude. Brigham Young University professor, Dr. Brent Top summarized, "One of the most important lessons I have learned through experience is that gratitude is an antidote to selfishness—counting blessings put problems and pains in perspective."[30] For instance, we could be mad at one of our children, or grateful that we have a child. We could be upset about the home we live in, or grateful we have a roof over our heads. We could be annoyed at our spouse for something we did that we did not agree with or be thankful that we have a spouse to come home to each night who will listen to us, love us, and nurture us.

President Dieter F. Uchtdorf reminded us that we could be grateful in any circumstance. Sometimes we may feel that life needs to be wonderful in order for us to be grateful. He explained, "It might sound contrary to the wisdom of the world to suggest that one who is burdened with sorrow should give thanks to God. But those who set aside the bottle of bitterness and lift instead the goblet of gratitude can find a purifying drink of healing, peace, and understanding."[31] In this same message, President Uchtdorf suggested, "instead of being thankful for things, we focus on being thankful in our circumstances—whatever they may be."[32]

Practicing Gratitude

We should pray each day for the gift of gratitude. We can ask God to help us see the blessings, gifts, and opportunities that he gives to us. Here are several helpful suggestions to make gratitude an important part of our lives and our family culture:

1. Keep a gratitude journal.

We can reflect on the blessings we have received, and rejoice in God's goodness in our lives as we prepare for bed each evening. In his research, Dr. Robert Emmons reported that people who regularly kept a gratitude journal and were in the habit of recognizing and expressing gratitude for their blessings reported feeling closer and more connected to people, had better relationships, were more likely to help others, felt less lonely, felt less depressed, slept better, and were more pleasant to be around."[33]

Think of three to five blessings you have experienced throughout the day or the week and record them in a gratitude journal. Look for blessings from the mundane to the magnificent. Before writing in his gratitude journal, President Henry B. Eyring pondered the following question: "Have I seen the hand of God reaching out to touch us or our children or our family today?[34] Here is a most helpful invitation that we would like you to consider. At the end of each day, respond to these four prompts in your journal:

1. Write about something funny that happened today
2. Write about a success that you had
3. Write about some things you are grateful for
4. Write about how you saw God's hand in your life today

As President Henry B. Eyring faithfully kept his gratitude journal, he said, "Something began to happen. As I would cast my mind over the day, I would see evidence of what God had done for one of us that I had not recognized in the busy moments of the day. As that happened, and it happened often, I realized that trying to remember had allowed God to show me what He had done."[35] This means that some of us would need to begin keeping a journal! It's never too late to begin a healthy, helpful practice.

2. Make a Gratitude Visit.

There are people in your life and in the lives of your family members who have made a big difference. Do they know the impact that they have made in your life? Do they realize how you feel about them? Have you thanked them lately? Consider parents, grandparents, friends, teachers, coaches, church leaders, and employers. Stop by their home and share your gratitude with them. Deliver a card or a note from your family. Bring some goodies over. Make a moment of it.

One of the most significant moments that Mark remembers was visiting his mission president before he passed away. Mark flew from Dallas to Salt Lake City for this visit and met up with two of his missionary companions. Although their mission president was quite weak from cancer, these former missionaries spent about an hour with him.

Since their missions had concluded thirty years earlier, these men had seen the hand of their mission president throughout their lives and wanted him to know of the impact he had on them and, consequently, on their families. These missionaries shared their deep feelings, their memories, and other life lessons. Each was serving in a bishopric at the time, and they recounted many lessons their mission president taught them about priesthood leadership. They also all had children serving in the mission field and related how the teachings of their mission president had blessed their families. Tears of joy and gratitude were shared freely. It was a moment that none present will ever forget. Their mission president passed away peacefully several weeks later.

3. Write a gratitude note or letter.

A note or a letter expressing gratitude is something the recipient can keep and hold onto forever. Sometimes, it may be easier to express something in writing. Moreover, writing something out can be especially beneficial if the recipient lives far away. When Mark was a missionary, serving in Seattle, Washington in the late 1980s, he broke his pelvis in a freak accident. While he lay in traction in the hospital for a couple of weeks, a kind, older couple from a local ward brought him a tape recorder and some cassette tapes of a man named William Wait. Brother Wait was a popular speaker in the Church back in those days, and his messages were just what the doctor ordered for a missionary in traction. Mark soaked up all of those messages that were full of faith, and hope, and optimism, and humor.

Once he was released from the hospital, he went to Deseret Book and purchased some William Wait tapes. Mark and his companions often listened to those tapes as they drove to their appointments and meetings. Years later, Mark was living with his wife and children in Mesa, Arizona, and William Wait was speaking at a fireside at a nearby chapel. Mark and his wife, Janie, arrived early, and at Janie's urging, Mark was able to approach Brother Wait before the meeting began. He thanked him for his messages on those tapes. Mark related how those talks brightened his days when everything seemed dark and dreary as he lay in traction at the hospital. Brother Wait was profusely humbled, and expressed his gratitude to Mark—for expressing gratitude.

Years later, Mark was living in the Dallas area with his family. At his work, he stumbled upon William Wait's mailing address. Again, he felt compelled to write Brother Wait a letter, expressing gratitude for his life and messages. Weeks later, Mark received a hand written message from Brother Wait, thanking him again, for expressing thanks. Two weeks later, Brother Wait passed away. Mark has always been grateful that he expressed appreciation and gratitude to a man who made a big difference in his life.

4. Expressing Prayers of Gratitude.

How often do we express gratitude in our prayers? Do we engage in that practice quickly, so we can get to the point of telling our Father in Heaven what we need? When was the last time you offered only a prayer of gratitude? Heavenly Father must love it when his children do not ask for anything but only express thanks, love, and appreciation. Elder Richard G. Scott taught, "I have saved the most important part about prayer until the end. It is gratitude. Our sincere efforts to thank our beloved Father generate wondrous feelings of peace, self-worth, and love. No matter how challenging our circumstances, honest appreciation fills our mind to overflowing with gratitude."[36] The expression of gratitude causes us to feel even more gratitude.

5. Teach your children to be grateful.

In our present world of selfishness and busyness, fewer and fewer children are taught the principle of gratitude. Often, parents give children in the neighborhood rides to and from school, to practices, recitals, and even Church meetings. Too often, such children never express thanks for the ride, or for kindnesses shown to them. Children receive Christmas gifts and birthday presents, and never write "thank you" notes to those who provided them with gifts. It becomes obvious that many children are not taught to express thanks—since they do not offer any. Teach your children to always express gratitude when someone does something for them. Encourage them to express gratitude in their prayers for their bounteous blessings, and to always express kindness, love, and appreciation for those who do kind things for them.

As we focus on our blessings, our circumstances, our faith, our families, and the gospel of Jesus Christ, we recognize that many are abundantly blessed. By recognizing our bounteous blessings, and by expressing gratitude to others and to our Father in Heaven, our stress and anxiety dissipate, and peace will enter our souls and calm our troubled hearts. Sit down today and make a list of each blessing you have. In fact, "Count your blessings; name them one by one. Count your many blessings; See what God hath done."[37]

References to Chapter 11

1   Dr. Robert A. Emmons, *Thanks! How Practicing Gratitude Can Make You Happier*, (Boston, Mass: Houghton Mifflin Company, 2007), 1.

2   As cited by Joseph B. Wirthlin, "Live in Thanksgiving Daily," BYU Speeches, 31 October 2000; https://speeches.byu.edu/talks/joseph-b-wirthlin/live-thanksgiving-daily/

3   Melody Beattie, *The Language of Letting Go: Daily Meditations on Codependency* (Center City, Minnesota: Hazelden, 1990), 218.

4   "Gratitude," Gospel Topics, churchofjesuschrist.org/study/manual/gospel-topics.

5   Janice Kaplan, "Gratitude Survey," *Conducted for the John Templeton Foundation*, June-October 2012.

6   Emmons, 5.

7   Emmons, 6.

8   Joseph F. Smith, *Gospel Doctrine*, 263.

9   As cited in Truman G. Madsen, *Joseph Smith the Prophet*, (Salt Lake City: Bookcraft, 1989), 104.

10   James E. Talmage, *Saturday Night Thoughts*, 483; as cited by Rulon T. Burton, *We Believe* (Salt Lake City: Tabernacle Books, 1994), 388.

11   Gordon B. Hinckley, *Conference Report*, October 1964, 117.

12   As cited by Joseph B. Wirthlin, "Live in Thanksgiving Daily," BYU Speeches, 31 October 2000, speeches.byu.edu.

13   Dennis Prager, *Happiness is a Serious Problem*, (New York: Harper Collins, 1998), 59.

14   David Steindl-Rast, *Gratefulness, the Heart of Prayer: An Approach to Life in Fullness*, (Ramsey, New Jersey: Paulist Press, 1984), 204.

15   Russell M. Nelson, "The Healing Power of Gratitude," https://assets.ldscdn.org/ac/ce/acce1d6a5b114c8c6eb33605830000a4176eb859/prayer_of_gratitude_video_and_awareness_materials.pdf

16   Robert A. Emmons, *Thanks! How Practicing Gratitude Can Make You Happier*, (Boston: Houghton Mifflin, 2007), 2.

17   Michael E. McCullough, Robert A. Emmons, and JoAnn Tsang, "The Grateful Disposition: A Conceptual and Empirical Topography," *Journal of Personality and Social Psychology* (2002), 82, 114; 188–199.

18   Dr. Robert Emmons, "Why Gratitude is Good," *Greater Good Magazine*; 16 November 2010; https://greatergood.berkeley.edu/article/item/why_gratitude_is_good

19   Kennon M. Sheldon and Sonja Lyubomirsky, "Achieving Sustainable New Happiness: Prospects, Practices, and Prescriptions." In A. Linley and S. Joseph (eds.), *Positive Psychology in Practice* (2004), 135–137.

20   Emmons, 2010.

21   Emmons, 2010.

22 A.M. Wood, J.J. Froh, & Adam W. A. Geraghty. "Gratitude and Well-Being. A Review and Theoretical Integration." *Clinical Psychology Review*, 30, no. 7, November 2010, 890–905.

23 Emmons, 2010, and Wood, et. al., 2010.

24 Robert A. Emmons, *Thanks! How Practicing Gratitude Can Make You Happier*, (Boston: Houghton Mifflin, 2007), 44.

25 This study was cited by Dr. Ray Huntington in his devotional address: "A Grateful Heart," BYU Speeches, 2 October 2012.

26 Thomas S. Monson, "An Attitude of Gratitude," *Ensign*, February 2000, 2.

27 Robert D. Hales, "Gratitude for the Goodness of God," *Ensign*, May 1992, 65.

28 Max Lucado, *Anxious for Nothing: Finding Calm in a Chaotic World*, (Nashville, Tenn.: Thomas Nelson, 2017), 95.

29 Lucado, 96.

30 Brent Top, *When You Can't Do It Alone* (Salt Lake City: Deseret Book, 2008), 13–14.

31 Dieter F. Uchtdorf, "Grateful in Any Circumstance," *Ensign*, May 2014.

32 Dieter F. Uchtdorf, "Grateful in Any Circumstance," *Ensign*, May 2014.

33 Robert A. Emmons, *Thanks! How Practicing Gratitude Can Make You Happier* (Boston: Houghton Mifflin, 2007), 44.

34 Henry B. Eyring, "O Remember, Remember," *Ensign*, November 2007, 67.

35 Eyring, 67.

36 Richard G. Scott, "Learning to Recognize Answers to Prayer," *Ensign*, November 1989, 32.

37 "Count Your Blessings," *Hymns*, no. 241.

Chapter 12

CHRISTLIKE ATTRIBUTES THAT HELP US OVERCOME FEAR AND ANXIETY

Doctrines believed and practiced do change and improve us, while ensuring our vital access to the Spirit. Both outcomes are crucial.

—Elder Neal A. Maxwell [1]

WE LIVE IN a world that changes rapidly. In fact, some could argue that the past twenty years have yielded unprecedented changes like in no other time in the world's history. We now have smartphones, computers, Wi-Fi, Bluetooth and many other technologies that we only dreamed of in the days of yesteryear. Ted and I remember when we were in middle school, and our teachers telling us that the day would come when we could have a television screen on our phone and would be able to view the person we would talk to on a screen. In those days, we visualized a large rotary phone with a ten-inch television screen on top of the base, for a grand total of about twenty pounds of plastic and aluminum. We could have never conceived of a smart phone weighing less than one-half pound and fitting in our pocket, with features such as Zoom and FaceTime that allow us to see the people with whom we are speaking.

Do you remember the days of the instamatic camera? We would pay a nice "chunk of change" for twelve exposures of film. Then we would selectively photograph twelve images. Next, we would drive our film to a "photo booth," which seemed to be in every grocery store parking lot in America. When the technology really ramped up, our film could be processed in twenty-four hours. Before those days, sometimes it took a week or two to have your film "developed." Finally, when you opened the envelope to view your pictures, perhaps only six or seven of the twelve you took even turned out. Compare that to the instantaneous photos we can now take with our phones and then instantly blast them out all over the world.

Modern technology has certainly made the world a better place. However, some of the changes that have occurred during the past thirty years are actually quite concerning. Crime rates, divorce rates, and unwed childbirths continue to climb. We are surrounded by a global pandemic, economic challenges, terrorism, wars, gangs, sexual perversion, pollution, hunger, famine, poverty,[2] and "spiritual wickedness in high places" (Ephesians 6:12). The world seems to become increasingly unsafe, and the love of many is waxing cold (Matthew 24:12). Elder Robert D. Hales summarized, "The world is moving away from the Lord faster and farther than ever before. The adversary has been loosed upon the earth."[3]

If there is any peace or consolation in these trends, it is that our Heavenly Father and Jesus Christ do not change. God is the same yesterday, today, and forever (Mormon 9:9). In fact, in the Book of Mormon, we learn that God changes not or He would cease to Be God (Mormon 9:19). No matter how crazy the world becomes, God the Father, and His Son, Jesus Christ are steady, sure, and secure. In them, there is no variability or changing (Mormon 9:9–10). We can all take great comfort in the truth that no matter how unstable and how variable the world becomes, God the Father and Jesus Christ are steadfast and immoveable. They do not change their minds or their hearts. Neither are they fickle, or affected by every societal whim or trend. There is great comfort and peace knowing these truths.

Many other divine attributes, principles, and gospel doctrines can provide an anchor to us in a world that changes each day. Elder Jeffrey R. Holland taught, "The solutions to life's problems are always gospel solutions."[4] We believe that peace comes from gospel living and drawing closer to Jesus Christ.

Doctrines that Help Us Overcome Fear and Anxiety

We belong to a Church and a gospel that teaches us to place fear, anxiety, and stress in their proper place. President Gordon B. Hinckley explained, "It is critical to recognize that fear comes not of God, but rather from the adversary."[5] Likewise, President Howard W. Hunter declared, "Fear, which can come upon people in difficult days, is a principle weapon in the arsenal which Satan uses to make mankind unhappy. He who fears loses strength for the combat of life in the fight against evil."[6] Where our Heavenly Father and Savior are full of life, light, hope, faith, and optimism, Satan is the author of darkness, doubt, despair, and fear.

Indeed, when we feel anxious or afraid, the Holy Ghost has a diminished role in our lives. The Spirit helps us to feel happy, joyful, and grateful, despite our circumstances. When we have the spirit of the Lord with us we feel light, love, and peace. God is not the author "of confusion, but of peace" (1 Corinthians 14:33). Elder Quentin L. Cook stated, "Emma Lou Thayne's beloved hymn asks the appropriate questions: 'Where can I turn for peace? Where is my solace when other sources cease to make me whole?' The answer is the Savior, who is the source and author of peace. He is the 'Prince of Peace.'"[7]

Christlike Attributes that Help Us Conquer Stress, Fear, and Anxiety

Jesus Christ can become our model for overcoming fear, anxiety, and stress. Often we emphasize the Savior's compassionate traits, such as healing the sick, forgiving sinners, and reaching out to the poor and downtrodden. Sometimes we forget that Jesus Christ was bold, fearless, and courageous. Simply put, Jesus Christ had no fear; he was the bravest being who ever walked the earth. Jesus boldly stood up to Satan, face to face. He rebutted every fiery dart that Satan threw at him with a scripture (See Matthew 4:1–11). Although many continually plotted against him, even seeking to kill him, Jesus continued to teach and influence his followers (John 5:16; Mark 7:5; Luke 13:31). Jesus Christ courageously stood up to the Pharisees and Sadducees, correcting their false doctrines and teachings (Mark 2:7; Mark 3:22; Luke 11:53–54). Christ stood up to the moneychangers who were desecrating the holy temple, and removed them from His Father's house (John 2; Matthew 21). There was a vicious mob who attempted to throw Jesus over a cliff, but he stood firm against them (Luke 4:28–29). He also stood up face-to-face and toe-to-toe with a mob who wanted to stone an adulterous woman (John 8). Even in the Garden of Gethsemane, he protected his disciples from a violent mob (John 18:8). Christ even stood up against Pilate, knowing that the Roman leader could have spared him (Matthew 27:1–26). Finally, Christ stood brave and firm as he was tortured and crucified (Matthew 27:27–50). Our Savior needs us to be courageous. We can learn much about courage and bravery as we study the life of our Savior, the Lord Jesus Christ.

Many years ago, President Henry D. Moyle explained, "Fear is a chief weapon of Satan in making mankind unhappy. He who fears loses strength for the combat of life, for the fight against evil. . . . As leaders in Israel, we must seek to dispel fear from among our people. A timid, fearing people cannot do their work well. . . . Latter day Saints . . . cannot afford to dissipate their strength in fear."[8]

We know that God reserved some of most courageous spirits to come to the earth in the last days. President George Q. Cannon taught, "God . . . reserved spirits for this dispensation who [would] have the courage and determination to face the world, and all the powers of the evil one" and who would "build up the Zion of our God, fearless of all consequences."[9] As parents, we have a responsibility of raising a generation of courageous youth, Helaman's warriors, if you will, to stand side by side with the Savior and to stare evil down like no other generation.

Besides looking at the Saviors' life, we can examine his attributes for strength to overcome our fears. Some of the attributes we will consider include faith, hope, and charity.

Faith

Faith in the Lord Jesus Christ is one of the most important tools in our arsenal to combat stress, fear, worry, doubt, and anxiety. In fact, in some respects we believe that anxiety is as much a spiritual issue as a mental or emotional problem. Sometimes those who fear or worry lack faith in the Lord in certain areas. It is not that they do not believe in Jesus Christ, or in the Restoration of the Gospel. However, when it comes to their own personal lives, they lack the faith that Jesus Christ will see them through their challenge, that Heavenly Father will assist them, or that their prayers will be heard and answered.

Sometimes when we experience anxiety, our faith is weakened. Do not misunderstand—our faith is often strong in other areas, but we may lack faith regarding the issues in our own lives—whether it be finances, our struggling child, health challenges, or a tenuous situation at work. However, those who may lack faith in their own lives may be able to muster enough faith to believe that our Father in Heaven will take care of similar issues for our next-door-neighbor. The challenge is to develop enough faith to genuinely believe that our Father in Heaven will help us face the obstacles in our lives and give us the strength to overcome them, or at least manage them.

Christian author Max Lucado explained that the most stressed out people "are control freaks. They fail at the quest they most pursue. The more they try to control the world, the more they realize they cannot. Life becomes a cycle of anxiety, failure; anxiety, failure; anxiety, failure. We can't take control because control is not ours to take."[10] Perhaps the opposite of "being filled with faith" is becoming overly controlling. Instead of having the faith and patience to wait for God's timing or His intervention in our lives, "controllers" take matters into their own hands. Such control is not necessarily manifest in the form of abuse or domination. Often control can be demonstrated in subtle, quite ways. For those who want control, what they really seem to wish for is that everything should work out their way. In fact, those who are controlling simply do not like surprises—they want life to be completely predictable. Nevertheless, faith is the remedy. If we have faith, we can turn things over to God and let him bear our burdens. In fact, we each can "cast [our] burdens on the Lord and trust his constant care."[11]

Too many of us let fear rule our lives. If someone we know is killed in a traffic accident on a particular stretch of highway, we vow that we will never drive on that road ever again. Sometimes we serve in the Church out of fear. What if we turned down a calling or a church assignment? Would that be a sentence straight to hell? Some of us parent out of fear—what if our children end up not serving a mission, not marrying in the temple, and leaving the Church at some point in their lives? Perhaps we see one of our toddler-aged grandchildren hit another young grandchild, and we automatically assume that our aggressive grandchild is on their way to prison. Sometimes we also work in our professions out of fear—what if I am terminated or blamed for something I did not do? We know of a man who will not allow his wife to respond or post on social media. He worries that his employer might "get wind" of his wife's post and terminate him.

Fear, if we let it, can become a dominating influence in our lives, affecting many of our moves and decisions. We should strive daily to replace fear with faith. Elder David A. Bednar once quoted Stonewall Jackson, who said, "Never take counsel from your fears." Elder Bednar then added, "To not take counsel from our fears means that faith in the Lord Jesus Christ overrules our fears and that we can press forward with a steadfastness in Him. To not take counsel from our fears means that we trust in God's guidance, assurance, and timing in our lives."[12]

If faith is such a key component in our battle against anxiety and fear, how do we build and increase our faith? First, faith is a "gift of God bestowed as a reward for personal righteousness."[13] If we want to build or increase our faith, we must live righteously, keeping our covenants and the commandments, and seeking for the spirit each day in our lives. Living righteously will build and increase our faith. Second, "faith comes by hearing the word of God."[14] If we want to increase our faith, we must immerse ourselves in God's word. This means that we should engage in a plan of daily scripture study, but also listening to and studying the words of our living prophets. Immersing ourselves on a diet of God's word can heal the wounded soul and bring peace, comfort, and tranquility to our lives. We can surround ourselves with wholesome and inspiring music. In essence, we can construct a faith-filled, Teflon-coated, spiritual environment where we can dwell. We can build a Zion in our own homes.

Hope

Along with faith, hope is necessary for us to move forward in our lives with confidence and courage. Satan would love nothing more than for you to give in to doubt and fear and to lose all hope. However, as members of the Church of Jesus Christ, we know that as long as God lives and Jesus is the Christ, hope will always be present. Elder John H. Groberg testified, "There is always hope. No matter how dismal things appear, no matter how problem prone we seem to be, no matter what reversals and setbacks we suffer, there is always hope. Hope is the thing that keeps up going."[15]

Elder Dieter F. Uchtdorf taught, "Hope is not knowledge, but rather the abiding trust that the Lord will fulfill His promises to us. It is confidence that if we live according to God's laws and the words of His prophets now, we will receive desired blessings in the future. It is believing and expecting that our prayers will be answered. It is manifest in confidence, optimism, enthusiasm, and patient perseverance."[16] As members of The Church of Jesus Christ of Latter-day Saints, we should be incurable optimists. Because the Holy Ghost can be our constant companion, we are enabled to be hopeful and conceive of the "best-case scenarios" in every situation. It is easy to be negative and critical in our modern era; indeed, there is no talent required to faultfind, criticize, or complain. However, the real test of our discipleship is whether or not we can be positive, hopeful, and optimistic when the storms rage around us.

At a recent General Conference, Elder Jeffrey R. Holland declared,

> So, when our backs are to the wall and, as the hymn says, "Other helpers fail and comforts flee," among our most indispensable virtues will be this precious gift of hope linked inextricably to our faith in God and our charity to others.
>
> In this bicentennial year, when we look back to see all we have been given and rejoice in the realization of so many hopes fulfilled, I echo the sentiment of a beautiful young returned sister missionary who said to us in Johannesburg just a few months ago, "[We] did not come this far only to come this far."
>
> "May we press forward with love in our hearts, walking in the "brightness of hope" that lights the path of holy anticipation we have been on now for 200 years. I testify that the future is going to be as miracle-filled and bountifully blessed as the

past has been. We have every reason to hope for blessings even greater than those we have already received because this is the work of Almighty God, this is the Church of continuing revelation, this is the gospel of Christ's unlimited grace and benevolence."[17]

We encourage you to pray for the gift of *hope*. Ask for the gift of optimism. Learn to see the good. Instead of viewing the glass as "half empty," learn to see it "half full." President Dieter F. Uchtdorf recently said, "Our best days are ahead of us, not behind us. . . . We are moving forward and upward to places we've never been, to heights we can hardly imagine. . . . Brothers and Sisters, with Christ at the helm, things will not only be all right; they will be unimaginable."[18]

Our living prophets speak with so much hope and conviction. A beginning place to cultivate hope is to believe in their words, and to believe in the promises God has given to us. We should pray to believe that "The future is as bright as your faith."[19] Open your patriarchal blessing and underline the promises the Lord has made to you—personally. Read the last General Conference proceedings and mark every promise the Lord has made to his people—collectively. We belong to a Church of hope. We should take comfort in a promise from the scriptures, quoted by Elder Jeffrey R. Holland. He said that we should be "filled with faith, and remember the Lord has said He "would fight [*our*] battles, [our] children's battles, and [the battles of our] children's children."[20] He also said, "It will be okay. Just be faithful. God is in charge. He knows your name and He knows your need."[21]

One of the best ways to conquer our fears and anxious thoughts is to develop hope in the future—hope for our individuals lives, for our families, friends, and neighbors. Do you want to cultivate greater hope? Elder M. Russell Ballard provided the formula. He taught, "I have learned over the years that our hope in Christ increases when we serve others. Serving as Jesus served, we naturally increase our hope in Him."[22]

Charity

Just as faith can overcome fear, charity or "the pure love of Christ" and fear are not compatible. In fact, fear causes us to become more self-focused while charity helps us to become more focused on others. We recognize this truth in our own lives. When we are anxious and fearful, we become preoccupied with our own issues and stressors—our deadlines at work, our concerns for our own health, our worry for those who violate our boundaries, our concerns for our own finances, and our worries about how the conditions of our nation will affect us. The list is continuous. Our fears can disconnect us from the Spirit of the Lord and, subsequently, from our loved ones. Perhaps this is why another "opposite" of fear is not just faith, but love. We know from the scriptures that "perfect love casteth out fear" (1 John 4:18), but why? Because when we love God and our neighbors, our focus becomes less on ourselves and more on others. The more we choose to focus on others, the less space there is to worry about ourselves.

Therefore, to combat our fears and worries, we should seek to cultivate a spirit of kindness and charity. Elder L. Tom Perry explained, "If we simply love God and love our neighbors, we are promised that we will overcome our fears."[23] Brigham Young University professor Brent Top explained how charity could pull us away from our own anxieties. He explained,

Serving the Lord by serving my fellowman, especially when I may feel least like doing so, is an important means whereby I am saved from my own self-centeredness and the distorted fixation on my own problems, pains, and inadequacies. I have learned that when I serve others—"succor the weak, lift up the hands which hang down, and strengthen the feeble knees" (D&C 81:5)—it is my hands that are lifted up and my knees that are strengthened.[24]

When we focus on other individuals, "there is less time to be concerned with ourselves."[25] President Gordon B. Hinckley believed that the best antidote for worry is work, and the best medicine for feelings of despair is service to others.[26] President Dieter F. Uchtdorf reminded us that if we are ever filled with fear and anxiety, we could become liberated from this fear by acquiring the pure love of Jesus Christ and focusing on the needs of others.[27] Perhaps President Lorenzo Snow provided the most specific counsel on this topic. He taught, "When you find yourselves a little gloomy, look around you and find somebody that is in a worse plight than yourself; go to him and find out what the trouble is, then try to remove it with the wisdom which the Lord bestows upon you; and the first thing you know, your gloom is gone, you feel light, the Spirit of the Lord is upon you, and everything seems illuminated."[28]

Mark shares a personal experience that highlights the concept that charity can be a wonderful antidote for anxiety, fear, and stress:

Back in the early 1990s, I was teaching seminary full-time and attending graduate school part-time. I was working on a master's degree in Educational Psychology at Northern Arizona University. At the time, NAU had a satellite program on the west side of Phoenix—Luke Air force Base to be exact. On several occasions, I had classes that were offered on Friday evenings and Saturday mornings. On a particular Saturday morning in the fall, following our Friday night classes, I got a late start for my morning class—it was usually about an hour drive from our home in East Mesa to the West Side of Phoenix. When I jumped into the car, the first thing I noticed was that the gas gauge was on empty, and I really needed to get gas. However, since I was already running late, I knew that if I stopped to get gas, I would be even later to my class. Besides, I felt that I probably had enough gas to get to class, and then on the way home I could fill the tank of the car.

As I remember, it was a stressful ride because I could not take my eyes off the gas gauge. As I entered the Phoenix area, I recognized my gas tank was on empty, but I assumed I could go for quite a way in my Subaru wagon with little gas in the tank. However, I was wrong. As I drove through the west side of Phoenix, perhaps about fifteen minutes from Luke Air Force Base, I ran out of gas. I was livid! I knew that this would be a big problem. I fully understood that by the time I walked to the gas station, borrowed a gas can, and then walked back to my car, put the gas in, and then drove back to the station to fill up, I would probably miss the first hour of my class—if not the first two hours.

Of course, as a certified worrier, I believed that being one-hour late to three-hour long class meant I would probably fail the mid-term, and consequently, fail the class. I would then have to take the class over, and then probably run out of gas again the following semester, and of course, I would fail the class again. I also believed because I ran out of gas, I would need to live like a hobo under a bridge for the rest of my life. That is how worriers think. Anyway, I began walking to the gas station, which was about one mile away. Once I arrived at the station, I borrowed a gas tank, filled it up, and then walked the mile back to my car. I put the gas in, got the car started, and then drove to the gas station to return the tank and fill my car up.

I was quite upset at myself by this point. I knew that I could have avoided this entire fiasco if I had just filled the car up with gas back on Friday evening in Mesa. But I decided to take a gamble and completely blew it. As I stood at the gas pump and filled my tank, I pondered how terrible my life was, and how being an hour late to a graduate class was about the worst thing that could happen to a human. I wondered what life would be like as a hobo, living under a bridge. As I was off in my thoughts about the unfairness of life, I recognized that someone was calling for me. I heard a voice saying something like, "Hey, could you help me?" I turned from the gas pump where I was standing, across the lane towards the next row of pumps. My eyes caught sight of the ugliest station wagon I have ever seen. At that point, I saw the man in the driver's seat, who looked like a cross between a Hell's Angel, a Pirate, Patches O'Houlihan, and someone who just escaped from prison. I went over to his car and leaned against the driver's side door to hear him more distinctly. He said, "Hey, could you help me fill up my car with gas." At first, I was a little leery of this man. I wandered if he was really a serial killer who wanted to throw me in his car, drive off into the desert, and shoot me. However, I felt he was harmless, so I said, "Sure, what do you need?" He then said, "Could you get my wheelchair down from the top of the car for me? Once you get it down, I can do the rest."

It did not take long to notice from the looks of his car that he probably lived in it. I felt embarrassed that I did not notice the huge wheelchair strapped to the top of his station wagon. I untied it, and then brought it down to the ground. I held the wheelchair *steady until he climbed in. As I was helping him towards the back of his vehicle, I noticed a bumper sticker on his car that read, "Vietnam Vet." It was then that I realized that this man was paralyzed because of an injury he received in the war.*

After helping him put gas in his car, and then tying his wheelchair back up to the top of his station wagon, I got back in my car and began the fifteen-minute drive to Luke Air Force base. At this point, I was well over an hour late for class. However, I do not remember if I ever felt happier driving to a college class. First, my happiness came from the simple act of serving someone in need. Second, my happiness came from my tremendous sense of gratitude. Here I was—a healthy, fully functioning LDS husband and father. I had a beautiful wife who I adored and three small children at the time—all healthy and happy. I had a home in a nice part of Mesa, Arizona. I had a car that did not look like a reject from a demolition derby. I had a job that I loved. I was in graduate school. I was an active and faithful member of The Church of Jesus Christ of Latter-day Saints—better yet—I had the restored gospel in my life.

After spending a few minutes with that Vietnam Vet, I knew my life was full, rich, and wonderful. I did not have anything to complain about—life was good. Walking into class late that day was not a problem at all. In fact, I realized later that I had learned much more at the gas station that day that I would that entire semester in graduate school.

When you begin to feel stress and the pressures of the world, learn to turn outward instead of inward. Find someone that you can help or bless. When we put others needs before our own, and serve and bless those around us, our own fears and problems seem to be put into proper perspective.

Faith, hope, and charity. These three great pillars of the gospel are the great antidote to stress, depression, fear, and anxiety. As you deepen your commitment to these principles and practices, you will feel the Lord's Spirit in your life, and you will begin to feel your load lighten. Your life will become much happier as you seek to lift the Spirits of those around you.

References to Chapter 12

1   Neal A. Maxwell, *One More Strain of Praise*, (Salt Lake City: Bookcraft, 1999), x.

2   Mark D. Ogletree, "Joseph Smith and the Spirit of Optimism," Religious Educator, Vol. 13, No.2, 2012, rsc.byu.edu/vol-13-no-2-2012/joseph-smith-spirit-optimism.

3   Robert D. Hales, "General Conference: Strengthening Faith and Testimony," *Ensign*, November 2013, 6–8.

4   Jeffrey R. Holland, "How Do I Love Thee?" BYU Speeches, 15 February 2000.

5   Gordon B. Hinckley, "God Hath Not Given Us the Spirit of Fear," *Ensign*, October 1984, 2.

6   Howard W. Hunter, *Teachings of Presidents of the Church: Howard W. Hunter* (2015), 70–71.

7   Quentin L. Cook, "Personal Peace: The Reward for Righteousness," *Ensign*, May 2013.

8   Henry D. Moyle, "Ye Shall Not Fear," Conference Report, October 1962, 86.

9   George Q. Cannon, *Journal of Discourses*, 26 Vols. (London: Latter-day Saints Book Depot, 1852–81), 11:230.

10 Max Lucado, *Anxious For Nothing: Finding Calm in a Chaotic World* (Nashville, Tenn.: Thomas Nelson, 2017), 24.

11 "How Gentle God's Commands," *Hymns*, no. 125.

12 David A. Bednar, "Fear Not, I am With Thee," *Church News*, December 26, 2012.

13 Bruce R. McConkie, *Mormon Doctrine*, 264.

14 Joseph Smith, *History of the Church*, 5:355.

15 John H. Groberg, "There is Always Hope," BYU Devotional and Fireside Speeches, 3 June 1984, 1.

16 Dieter F. Uchtdorf, "The Infinite Power of Hope," *Ensign*, November 2008.

17 Jeffrey R. Holland, "A Perfect Brightness of Hope," *Ensign*, May 2020; emphasis added.

18 Dieter F. Uchtdorf, "God Will Do Something Unimaginable," *Ensign*, November 2020.

19 Thomas S. Monson, "Be of Good Cheer," *Ensign*, May 2009.

20 Jeffrey R. Holland, "The Ministry of Angles," *Ensign*, November 2008, 29–31.

21 Jeffrey R. Holland, "Terror, Triumph, and a Wedding Feast," CES Fireside, 12 September 2004.

22 M. Russell Ballard, "Hope in Christ," *Ensign*, May 2021.

23 L. Tom Perry, "Perfect Love Casteth Out Fear," *Ensign*, November 2011.

24   Brent Top, *When You Can't Do it Alone* (Salt Lake City: Deseret Book, 2008), 53.

25   Spencer W. Kimball, "Small Acts of Service," *Ensign*, December 1974, 2.

26   Gordon B. Hinckley, *Teachings of Gordon B. Hinckley*, 595–596.

27   Dieter F. Uchtdorf, "Perfect Love Casteth Out Fear," *Ensign*, May 2017.

28   Lorenzo Snow, Conference Report, 6 Apr. 1899, 2–3.

Chapter 13

LAUGHTER IS STILL THE
BEST MEDICINE

Happiness is the object and design of our existence.

—Joseph Smith [1]

WITHOUT QUESTION, THE world is more anxiety-filled and more stressful than it has been in a long time. We live in an age of plagues, viruses, political unrest, social divisions, and economic uncertainty. In order to survive the toxic and wicked environment we live in, we will need, among other things, a healthy dose of Vitamin H—Humor! All of us need to laugh more—at each other and ourselves. We need to be able to find the humor in everyday situations that would otherwise be viewed as stressful.

Consider the following experience. J. Golden Kimball was a General Authority who was beloved by many because of his amazing sense of humor and his colorful vocabulary. Elder Kimball was walking on the streets of Salt Lake City during a winter snowstorm, just a couple of weeks before Christmas. As he was crossing the street at South Temple, preparing to walk into the north door of ZCMI, a woman carrying an armload of packages burst through the doors. As Elder Kimball gingerly walked across the snow and ice, he was met head-on by this woman whose visibility was blocked by the load she was carrying. When the two collided, packages flew everywhere, and the woman landed right on top of the slender General Authority. After landing on Elder Kimball, the pair began sliding towards the curb. Author James Kimball continued the story:

All traffic stopped. Everyone stood entranced by the most unlikely sight. They slid until they hit the curb. It was then that the woman realized someone was beneath her. She brushed the snow away and exclaimed, "Oh, Brother Kimball, it's you! Speak to me. Are you all right?" "It's all right, Sister, but you'll have to get off here," he painfully croaked. "This is as far as I go."[2]

We assume that most people in Salt Lake City never imagined seeing a woman riding on top of a General Authority, on a sheet of ice, across the busiest street in town! That had to be both shocking and humorous for all who had eyes to see! Perhaps this story was shared that evening in the homes of those who witnessed that awkward experience. Maybe someone who was especially stressed over the approaching Christmas holidays found some delight and relief when they saw Elder Kimball and the woman crash into each other. If we do not find the humor in our daily lives, humor will most likely find us. In fact, humor is most often around us—we simply need to look for it. Some will have to look harder than others do, but humor is there—somewhere! Discovering the humor in daily life is one of the most powerful ways to cope with the stresses and strains life has to offer. Humor certainly has a way of reducing fear, stress, anxiety, worry, anger, and depression.

This is perhaps why many believe that *laughter is the best medicine.* There is wisdom in not taking ourselves too seriously, laughing despite our problems, and seeing the humor in most things that we do. Many experts over the years have suggested that no matter what the crisis is in our lives, if we can look back on our problems weeks, months, or even years later, we most likely could find some humor in the situation.

For example, Mark remembers an experience when he and his family were driving from Houston, Texas to Mesa, Arizona after the Christmas Holidays. He had expected to drive all through the night while his wife, Janie, and their three small children slept peacefully in the car. However, Mark became completely exhausted by the time they reached Junction, a small town in West Texas. He woke Janie up to explain that they would need to find a hotel because Mark could no longer drive without falling asleep at the wheel. As you could imagine, there were not many hotel choices in Junction, Texas at 1:00 a.m. After trying to find a vacancy in several normal hotels, they were forced to settle with the worst, flea-ridden, filthy hotel they had ever encountered. The beds were covered in hair and dirt. The room was filthy and smelled like a pigpen. To make a long story short, it was a miserable night at the "Bates Motel." Although Mark slept like a baby (the hotel was not much different from a few of his missionary apartments), Janie could not sleep a wink. She thought that she heard mice crawling across the floor during the night, and was sure a serial killer was going to break through the door at any moment.

That experience occurred many years ago. The three small children that slept soundly in the flea-ridden hotel are now all grown and have children of their own. Mark and Janie can now laugh about that experience years later—but they certainly were not laughing when they stayed there. All of us have had many similar experiences. Things that may appear to be a crisis can actually be viewed through the lens of humor a little later down the road.

The Doctrine of Humor

On January 14, 1847, the Lord gave counsel and direction to Brigham Young, who was about to lead a massive migration across the plains. This revelation is found in section 136 of the Doctrine and Covenants. In verse 28, the Saints were commanded to praise the Lord with singing and dancing on the journey.

Why? Imagine what life would be like, riding in a wagon, walking, or dealing with children for 10–12 hours a day. After the evening meal, wouldn't you feel exhausted? Consider the balance that singing and dancing could provide a group of beleaguered, exhausted Saints. These people certainly needed some fun and humor in their lives, and singing and dancing could certainly provide that!

Is our Father in Heaven funny? Does He have a sense of humor? We believe that He does. President Heber C. Kimball taught that our Heavenly Father "is a cheerful, pleasant, lively, and good natured being."[3] We can assume that our Father in Heaven is a joyful, happy being, who relishes life, sees the humor in things, and loves to laugh. If we are created in his image, and we laugh often, what should we conclude about our Father in Heaven's sense of humor? Lehi taught that, "men are, that they might have joy" (2 Nephi 2:25). Who revealed that to Lehi? Our Father in Heaven wants all of us to have joy because He has joy! Randy Alcorn, an evangelical Christian author, wrote:

> In Heaven, I believe our joy will often erupt in laughter. When laughter is prompted by what is appropriate, God always takes pleasure in it. I think Christ will laugh with us, and his wit and fun-loving nature will be our greatest sources of endless laughter. Where did humor originate? Not with people, angels, or Satan. God created all good things, including good humor. If God did not have a sense of humor, human beings as his image-bearers wouldn't either. . . . God made us to laugh and to love to laugh.[4]

Joseph Smith was also a man who possessed a great sense of humor. He sought out jovial company, was often the life of the party, and possessed a "native cheery temperament."[5] Dr. Truman G. Madsen described Joseph as "a hail-fellow-well-met, easily inclined to laughter, sociable, animated, the life of the party, and colorful in his use of language."[6] Joseph was always able to cope with the challenges of life with a healthy dose of humor. On 7 July 1843, Joseph wrote in his journal, "In the evening I received an extremely saucy and insulting letter from R.D. Foster. Pleasant evening."[7] On another occasion, word arrived in Nauvoo that Porter Rockwell had been arrested for shooting ex-Missouri Governor, Lilburn W. Boggs. Joseph responded, "Port couldn't have done it. He wouldn't have missed."[8] Latter-day Saint historian, Dr. Leonard J. Arrington explained,

> The Prophet recognized as unhealthy the mind that lacked balance, perspective, and humor. In the society of his day there were many earnest people who habitually looked on the serious side of things that had no serious side, who regarded humor as incompatible with religion. . . . But Joseph Smith saw humor and religion as quite reconcilable. As he saw it, once one acknowledges that there is something beyond laughter—a

core of life that is solemn, serious, and tender—there is still plenty of room for jesting. At least, that is the way he was—'a jolly good fellow' as one contemporary described him.[9]

President Spencer W. Kimball was also known for his keen sense of humor and quick wit. Once while in the nation's capital for the dedication of the Washington D.C. Temple, President Kimball was invited to the United States Senate floor to offer the invocation prior to a session. Unfortunately, many senators that particular morning were involved in other committee meetings. Therefore, few were in the senate chamber when it came time for the Prophet to pray. Someone apologized to President Kimball for the lack of attendance during his prayer. The Prophet quipped, "That's all right. I was not going to pray to them, anyway."[10] President Kimball was always quick on his feet regarding his "one-liners." Once, his Sister Alice came to visit him. She gave him a kiss, and then she greeted all of the other people who were in the room. Then she came back to her brother, kissed him again, and asked, "Did I kiss you already?" President Kimball replied, "The first time must not have impressed you that much." In his later years, a relative greeted President Kimball by asking, "Do you know who I am?" The Prophet replied, "If you don't know who you are, how do you expect me to remember?"[11] No wonder Elder Boyd K. Packer once stated, "A good sense of humor is a characteristic of a well-balanced person. It has always been apparent that the prophets were men with very alert and pleasing senses of humor."[12] If such a sense of humor is appropriate for the Lord's prophets, it should be appropriate for each of us!

President Gordon B. Hinckley once declared, "We've got to have a little humor in our lives. You had better take seriously that which should be taken seriously but, at the same time, we can bring in a touch of humor now and again. If the time ever comes when we can't smile at ourselves, it will be a sad time."[13] Sister Marjorie Pay Hinckley was just as funny as her husband, Gordon. She once explained,

> Another thing that we tried to do is not take ourselves too seriously. You get into a lot of trouble when you do that. I tried to laugh instead of cry when you felt like crying. It was always better to laugh, [like] the day I took a beautiful casserole from

the oven and my six-year-old boy said, "Mom, how come you baked the garbage?" Children are like that. There are days when it is hard to laugh.[14]

Sister Hinckley became famous for saying, "The only way to get through life is to laugh your way through it. You either have to laugh or cry. I prefer to laugh. Crying gives me a headache."[15] The late Richard L. Evans stated, "Humor is essential to a full and happy life. It is a reliever and a relaxer of pressure and tension, and the saving element in many situations."[16]

Humor is, in many ways, the spice of life. Laughter and humor can heal our wounded souls and bring peace and contentment into our hearts. Joseph F. Smith explained, "I do not believe the Lord intends and desires that we should pull a long face and look sanctimonious and hypocritical. I think he expects us to be happy and of a cheerful countenance."[17] Parents not only have a responsibility to create a home environment where the Spirit of the Lord can reside but where happiness and laughter prevails.

For example, when Mark's wife, Janie, was a teenager, she began to resist going on dates. Her home was fun, full of laughter, and happiness. While on dates with young men, she longed to be back home—she felt she was missing all the fun and excitement. Most children want to be in homes where there is laughter, happiness, and fun. President Ezra Taft Benson suggested that all parents should provide a home where a happy and positive influence can exist. He then said, "In future years the costliness of home furnishings or the number of bathrooms will not matter much, but what will matter significantly is whether our children felt love and acceptance in the home. *It will matter greatly whether there was happiness and laughter, or bickering and contention.*"[18]

Laughter is Good Medicine

Humor is certainly good medicine. It is crucial for our survival in a wicked, toxic, busy, stress-filled world. Laughter can help us to see the lighter side of difficult situations. Laughter can relieve our stress, anxiety, and depression. We know that humor can help us, heal us, and help put our problems in perspective. A healthy sense of humor can help us navigate our way through difficult times, and can certainly lift the spirits of others. During the present times, a healthy sense of humor will help us through the challenges we face.

In his book, *Anatomy of Illness*, Norman Cousins had some interesting thoughts on humor. Cousins understood that "A merry heart doeth good like a medicine" (Proverbs 17:22). In his book, Cousins wrote,

> The Bible tells us that a merry heart works like a doctor. Exactly what happens to the human mind and body as the result of humor is difficult to say. But the evidence that it works has stimulated the speculations not just of physicians but of philosophers and scholars over centuries: . . . humor purges the blood, making the body young, lively, and fit. . . . It has always seemed to me that hearty laughter is a good way to jog internally without having to go outdoors.[19]

Indeed, humor gives your brain a workout! The frontal lobe moves from information processing towards an emotional response when laughter occurs.[20] Laughter also releases chemicals such as dopamine, which enhances pleasure; serotonin, which lightens our mood; and endorphins, which make us feel so much better![21] A study conducted at Vanderbilt University demonstrated that ten to fifteen minutes of laughter could burn up to forty calories.[22] So, start "laughing off" those extra pounds.

Furthermore, many academic studies that have shown that humor and laughter help people live longer and happier lives. Those with a healthy sense of humor are more creative and productive, they have more energy, and they experience less stress and anxiety. Did you know that when a person laughs, "their blood pressure decreases, heart rate and respiration increase, the body releases endorphins, and depressions declines. After the laughter subsides and you relax again, the good feeling has a lasting effect, even until the next day. Not many medicines will do that."[23]

A wealth of research that has documented the benefits of humor and laughter. Consider the following *mental health benefits*:

- Laughter can increase personal life satisfaction, and makes it easier to cope with difficult situations.[24]
- In a study by Seppälä, laughter was shown to decrease stress, regulate emotions, help with learning engagement, and can sharpen an individual's ability to remember things.[25]
- In Yim's study, laughter and humor correlated with enhanced mental functioning, reduction of stress, anxiety, and tension. In addition, humor elevates moods, self-esteem, hope, energy, and vigor.[26]
- Other studies have demonstrated that laughter and humor are directly linked to reducing loneliness and psychological distress. Humor also improves mental functioning, life functioning, quality of life, and is correlated with satisfaction and pleasure in life.[27]

A significant amount of research has also shown the relationship between laughter, humor, and physical health. For example, researchers at the Mayo Clinic have demonstrated that laughter can stimulate many organs. Laughter also enhances an individual's intake of oxygen and stimulates ones heart, lungs, and muscles. Laughter and humor also increase endorphins in our blood system.[28] Researchers at the Mayo Clinic have also shown that laughter can be a catalyst for circulation and muscle relaxation, which can reduce physical symptoms of stress.[29] Consider some other physical health benefits:

- Laughter can lower inflammation, increase good cholesterol, and decrease the production of cortisol.[30] Cortisol is the fuel for anxiety.
- In another study, Fujiwara and Okamura reported that laughter relaxes the nervous system.[31]
- Yim showed that laughter relaxes the muscles in the body, improves respiration, stimulates circulation, decreases stress hormones, and increases the immune system's defenses, elevates the pain threshold and tolerance, increases blood serotonin levels, strengthens the immune system, reduces blood pressure, and decreases stress hormones.[32]

Researchers have also examined the social benefits to laughter and humor. For instance, laughter can build and strengthen relationships,[33]increase relationship satisfaction, and facilitate group cohesion.[34] It also increases social bonds, enhances attraction to a romantic partner,[35] increases friendliness and helpfulness, improves interpersonal interactions, and can increase social support.[36] Undoubtedly, laughter is the best medicine! And, if you do not agree with that, at least it can be the *cheapest* prescription in your medicine cabinet!

Suggestions to Incorporate Laughter More in Your Life

There are many things we can do to in our lives to laugh more often. Our list is not comprehensive, but here are some suggestions.

1. *Try to smile every day, and make others smile as well.* Smiling is a sign that we are happy. Sometimes, just smiling at others can brighten their day as well. Remember, "A merry heart maketh a cheerful countenance" (Proverbs 15:13).

2. *Surround yourself with some funny people.* If you meet a funny person, or know of a funny couple in your neighborhood or community, get to know them. Associate with them often. Their humor will most likely rub off on you. Try to associate with people who give off positive energy. Avoid those who are so negative that they can suck the life out of you!

3. *Watch funny television shows and movies.* Too many people go to bed watching the news. Can there be anything more depressing than that? If you have time to watch some television, engage in programs that are wholesome, and that can make you laugh. To prepare for a healthy night of sleep, laughter can be just what the doctor ordered.

4. *Identify clean, wholesome comedians to listen to or watch.* Great comedians can make us laugh at the everyday challenges and experiences life has to offer. When driving in the car or while hanging out with the family in the evening, sometimes

it can be fun to listen to a clean comedian, like Brian Regan, or Tim Hawkins. *Dry Bar Comedy* is an app that features clean comedians.

5. ***Capture the funny stories in your life by writing them down***. When was the last time you wrote down something funny that happened? Funny things happen all the time. Why not create a journal, or even a book that can be shared with your family, of the funny events that have happened in your life? Do your children or grandchildren say funny things? Then write them down! Share these stories at the dinner table and around the campfire. Such stories and experiences can heal the wounded soul and bring joy and happiness into our lives!

6. ***Try to find the humor in everyday events***. Years ago, Mark was talking with a family member who said, "Nothing funny ever happens in my life. I guess I just have a boring existence." This is highly unlikely. The key to the happy life is knowing how to look for humor. Train your eyes and your mind to look for the humor in life—because it is there. Learn to find the humor in everyday events.

7. ***Share funny and humorous stories with your family***. It is fun, and therapeutic, to sit around the dinner table, the campfire, or in your favorite family gathering place and share humorous stories and experiences with each other. Not only are these stories healing for the soul, but they should be passed down from one generation to the next. What could be better than a night of laughter with your family? We know of some parents who, at the end of each day, have each family member share something funny that happened that day.

Jim Valvano was a famous college basketball coach back in the late 1970s and early 1980s. In 1983, he coached the North Carolina State Wolfpack to a miraculous win over the highly favored Houston Cougars to claim the National Championship. Known as Coach "V" to everyone around him, he loved and inspired his players to heights they never imagined. Unfortunately, just a few years after leaving coaching, Jimmy V was diagnosed with an aggressive form of cancer in 1992.

Almost two months before his premature death, Jimmy V, a man riddled with cancer throughout his body, attended the first ESPY Awards at Madison Square Garden. He was there to accept the first Arthur Ashe Courage and Humanitarian Award. Jimmy V was so sick and weak that many did not know how he would have the energy to climb the steps to the dais to accept the award. However, Coach Valvano miraculously made it to the podium to give one of the most inspirational speeches in human history. Among many other things said, Jimmy V gave this recommendation:

> To me, there are three things we all should do every day. . . . Number 1 is laugh. You should laugh every day. Number 2 is think. You should spend some time in thought. Number 3 is you should have your emotions moved to tears, could be happiness or joy. But think about it. If you laugh, you think and you cry, that's a full day. That's a heckuva day. You do that seven days a week, you're going to have something special.[37]

Laughing each day helped Jimmy V through the most significant trial of his life. Daily laughter can also help each of us as we navigate our way through this fallen world. Heavenly Father wants his children to have joy and happiness, despite the stresses and strains of life. Laughter can indeed be the very best medicine. Learn how to create a culture of humor and laughter in your home, and pass that legacy down to your children.

References to Chapter 13

1 *Teachings of the Prophet Joseph Smith*, sel. Joseph Fielding Smith (1976), 255–256.

2 James Kimball, *J. Golden Kimball Stories: Mormonism's Colorful Cowboy*, (Salt Lake City: White Horse Books, 1999), 90.

3 Heber C. Kimball, *Deseret News*, 25 February 1957; as cited in Brad Wilcox, "If We Can Laugh at It, We Can Live with It," *Ensign*, March 2000.

4 Randy Alcorn, *50 Days of Heaven*, (Carol Stream, Ill.: Tyndale House Publishers, 2006), Day 43.

5 Joseph Smith History, 2:28.

6 Truman G. Madsen, *Joseph Smith the Prophet*, (Salt Lake City: Bookcraft, 1989), 25.

7 *Joseph Smith Papers*, History, 1 May 1844 to 8 August 1844, 71; as cited by Dr. Jeffrey Marsh, "How Joseph's Native Cheery Temperament" Sustained Him Through Trials," 7 May 2019; https://latterdaysaintmag.com/how-joseph-smiths-native-cheery-temperament-sustained-him-through-trials/

8 Cited in Nicholas Van Alfen, *Porter Rockwell—Mormon Frontier Marshall*, 1964, 21; as cited by Marsh.

9 Leonard J. Arrington, "Joseph Smith and the Lighter View," *New Era*, August 1976, 10.

10 Edward L. Kimball, "Spencer W. Kimball: A Man of Good Humor," *BYU Studies*, Vol. 25, 1985.

11 Edward L. Kimball, "Spencer W. Kimball: A Man of Good Humor," *BYU Studies*, Vol. 25, 1985.

12 Boyd K. Packer, *Teach Ye Diligently* (Salt Lake City: Deseret Book, 1975), 249.

13 Gordon B. Hinckley, *Teachings of Gordon B. Hinckley*, (Salt Lake City: Deseret Book, 1997), 432.

14 Marjorie Pay Hinckley, BYU Women's Conference, 2 May 1996; see also Marjorie Hinckley in *Glimpses into the Life and Heart of Marjorie Pay Hinckley*, ed. Virginia H. Pearce (Salt Lake City: Deseret Book, 1999), 61.

15 Marjory Pay Hinckley, *Small and Simple Things* (Salt Lake City: Deseret Book, 2003). 126.

16 Richard L. Evans, *Improvement Era*, February 1968, 71.

17 Joseph F. Smith, Jr., Conference Report, October 1916, 70.

18 Ezra Taft Benson, *Ensign*, April 1981, 34.

19 Norman Cousins, *Anatomy of an Illness*, (New York: W.W. Norton & Company, 2005), 93–94.

20 Scott Edwards, "Humor, Laughter, and Those Aha Moments," *On the Brain*, 16, no. 2, Spring 2010.

21   Edwards.

22   Clinton Colmenares, "No Joke: Study Finds Laughing Can Burn Calories," *Reporter* (6 June 2005).

23   Gary K. Palmer, "The Power of Laughter," *Ensign*, September 2007.

24   Mayo Clinic Staff, "Stress Relief From Laughter? It's Not a Joke," Mayo Clinic, 26 June, 2019.

25   Emma Seppälä, "Laughing Can Boost Health, Learning, and More," *Psychology Today* (Sussex Publishers, March 26, 2020), https://www.psychologytoday.com/us/blog/feeling-it/202003/laughing-can-boost-health-learning-and-more.

26   JongEun Yim, "Therapeutic Benefits of Laughter in Mental Health: A Theoretical Review," *Tohoku J Exp. Med.*, July 2016, 243–49, https://doi.org/https://doi.org/10.1620/tjem.239.243.

27   Gonot-Schoupinsky, Freda N., Gulcan Garip, and David Sheffield. "Laughter and Humour for Personal Development: A Systematic Scoping Review of the Evidence." *European Journal of Integrative Medicine* (August 2020), 37, https://doi.org/10.1016/j.eujim.2020.101144.

28   Mayo Clinic, 2019.

29   Mayo Clinic, 2019.

30   Seppälä.

31   Fujiwara, Y., & Okamura, H, "Hearing laughter improves the recovery process of the autonomic nervous system after a stress-loading task: A randomized controlled trial," *BioPsychoSocial Med*, 12, 22 (2018).

32   Yim.

33   Seppälä.

34   Martin, Rod A., and Thomas E. Ford. "The Social Psychology of Humor," essay in *The Psychology of Humor: An Integrative Approach*, 2nd ed., 247–82. The New Yorker, 2018.

35   Martin.

36   Yim.

37   Jimmy V's Speech, Thursday, March 4, 1993, first ESPY Awards at Madison Square Garden; emphasis added, https://www.espn.com/espn/feature/story/_/id/24087641/jimmy-v-espys-speech-annotated.

Chapter 14

LOOKING UP

Two men looked out from prison bars,
one saw the mud, the other saw stars.

—Dale Carnegie[1]

SEVERAL YEARS AGO, Elder Carl B. Cook of the Quorum of the Seventy shared the following experience. After his first week as a newly called General Authority, he left his office after a long day, overwhelmed with some of the challenges of his new assignment. As he walked towards the elevator at the Church Administration Building, he thought to himself, "How can I possibly do this?" Elder Cook then explained,

> As the elevator descended, my head was down and I stared blankly at the floor. The door opened and someone entered, but I didn't look up. As the door closed, I heard someone ask, "What are you looking at down there?" I recognized that voice—it was President Thomas S. Monson. I quickly looked up and responded, "Oh, nothing." (I'm sure that clever response inspired confidence in my abilities!) But he had seen my subdued countenance and my heavy briefcase. He smiled and lovingly suggested, while pointing heavenward, "It is better to look up!" As we traveled down one more level, he cheerfully explained that he was on his way to the temple.

When he bid me farewell, his parting glance spoke again to my heart, "Now, remember, it is better to look up."[2]

By figuratively looking up, focusing on the positive, and ignoring the negative, we can improve our lives and increase our overall well-being and quality of life. As mental health professionals, we have come to understand that an individual's quality of life is often determined by what they choose to *focus* on. In fact, it seems that a happy life boils down to focusing on the cheerful, healthy, and positive experiences that surround us. We agree with President Thomas S. Monson—it is better to look up. Unfortunately, many individuals in this world and in the Church choose to consistently focus on the wrong things. Instead of looking up, their eyes are often firmly fixed on the ground. Some spend their entire existence worried and concerned about the terrible conditions in the world, such as politics, terrorism, and natural disasters. Others are more focused on their personal problems, such as their finances, children, career advancement, health issues, and their social lives. Unfortunately, too many of these individuals too often do not see the positive and joyful experiences that life has to offer. Over time, their negative focus on life leads to anxiety, depression, stress, and much unhappiness.

A Lesson from Florence Chadwick

Let us consider an example of how an improper focus can alter and change the outcomes we desire. Perhaps some of you have heard of a woman named Florence Chadwick. Florence was a famous swimmer back in the 1950s. However, she was not keen on swimming in pools; instead, she enjoyed "open-water" swimming. Florence loved to swim across lakes, rivers, ship channels, and oceans. On August 8, 1950, at the age of thirty, she swam the twenty-three-mile English Channel, from France to England, in thirteen hours and twenty minutes, breaking the current women's record. Then, just one year later, Florence crossed the English Channel again, swimming this time from England to France, completing her swim in sixteen hours and twenty-two minutes, making her the first woman to swim the English Channel in both directions. Obviously, Florence was a strong and courageous swimmer, which made the next major swimming event in her life even more interesting.

On July 4, 1952, at the age of thirty-four, Florence attempted to swim the twenty-six miles between Catalina Island and the California coastline—often called the Catalina Channel. Her goal was to be the first woman to swim that specific span of ocean. As she began her swim from Catalina Island, she was flanked by small boats that watched for sharks and were prepared to help her if she got hurt or grew tired. On this particular day, the sea was like an ice bath and the fog became so dense that she could barely see her support boats. To make matters worse, sharks often cruised towards her, so the men in the boats fired rifle shots to scare them away.

Shark-infested waters, dense fog, and frigid water temperatures would appear to be a good reason to stay home and enjoy the Fourth of July festivities from your lawn chair in the front yard. Not surprisingly, after about fifteen hours of swimming in these terrible conditions, Florence began to doubt her ability, and she told her mother, who was in one of the boats, that she did not think she could make it. Nevertheless, her mother begged her to not give up. Florence swam for another hour before asking to be pulled out, unable to see the coastline due to the fog.

As she sat in the boat, she discovered that she had stopped swimming just a half mile away from her destination. Yes, she had swum twenty-five and a half miles, and then essentially "pulled the plug," when she was so close as to practically hear the waves crashing on the shore. At a news conference the following day, Florence said, "All I could see was the fog. I think if I could have seen the shore, I would have made it." Florence did not reach the shoreline because of her lack of single-mindedness—instead of focusing on the approaching shoreline, she chose to zoom in on the fog.

Two months later, Florence tried again. The same thick fog set in, but she succeeded in reaching Catalina. On this second attempt, she said that she kept a mental image of the shoreline in her mind while she swam. She attributed her success to her "laser-focus" on the shoreline, which helped her win the coveted prize of accomplishment. The visualization of her goal allowed her to accomplish an almost impossible feat. Florence later swam the Catalina channel on two additional occasions. Incidentally, she eclipsed the men's record by more than two hours.[3]

In our mental health careers and in our ecclesiastical responsibilities, we have seen many individuals over the years who have become too focused on the fog in their lives: the hurts and pains they have experienced; built-up anger and resentment toward those who have injured them; their own mistakes, inadequacies, and weaknesses; and uncertainties and fears about the future. Consequently, many of these individuals end up spiraling into bouts of depression, anxiety, and stress because of their fixation on unhelpful things. *Life really is all about what you decide to focus on.*

Walking on the Water

Many of us are familiar with some of the events that occurred in Matthew 14—especially of Peter walking on the water. You may remember that Jesus had gone into the mountains to pray (Matthew 14:23) while his disciples were in a ship, heading to the other side of the Sea of Galilee (Matthew 14:22). When the ship reached the middle of the sea, a storm blew in, and the conditions became quite treacherous. To comfort his disciples, Jesus simply walked "on the sea" (Matthew 14:25) to minister to his friends. Assuming that Jesus was a Spirit, the disciples were deathly afraid, and "they cried out for fear" (Matthew 14:26). Likewise, each of us have fears, worries, and concerns. Many of us, like the Savior's disciples, are afraid of things that we do not understand or comprehend. And Jesus cries out to each of us, "Be of good cheer; it is I; be not afraid" (Matthew 14:27).

Nevertheless, as soon as Peter recognized that it was Jesus who was walking on the sea, he wanted to engage in an incredible opportunity. Peter asked the Savior if he could walk on the water toward him (Matthew 14:29). Often, we forget that Peter walked on a boisterous sea longer than any of us ever have! Even so, after walking a short distance, he began to notice the wind and the waves, and soon began to sink. He cried out, "Lord, save me" (Matthew 14:30), which Jesus gladly did. The Savior grabbed Peter's hand, chided him for his lack of faith, and they walked back to the ship together—on the water! It wasn't until then, that the wind stopped blowing (Matthew 14:31–32).

It was Peter's lack of focus that got him into trouble. When he took his eyes off the Savior, he began to sink into the water. Indeed, when he considered that he was in the middle of the Sea of Galilee in a raging storm, and then focused on the wind, and water, and waves that were drenching his robes, he began to panic. In defense of Peter, we are certain that most of us would have reacted in a similar fashion. President Howard W. Hunter, speaking of this experience with Jesus and Peter, taught:

> Only when with wavering faith he removed his glance from the Master did he begin to sink. It is my firm belief that if as individual people, as families, communities, and nations, we could, like Peter, fix our eyes on Jesus, we too might walk triumphantly over the swelling waves of disbelief and remain unterrified amid the rising winds of doubt. But if we turn away our eyes from him in whom we must believe, as it is so easy to do and the world is so much tempted to do, if we look to the power and fury of those terrible and destructive elements around us rather than to him who can help and save us, then we shall inevitably sink in a sea of conflict and sorrow and despair.[4]

Like Peter, who walked briefly on the water—Florence Chadwick *also* took her eyes off her goal, and chose to focus on the many distractions that surrounded her. Instead of keeping her eyes firmly fixated on the shore, she became more attentive to the fog and the frigid waters. Remember, "Where there is no vision, the people perish" (Proverbs 29:18). In order to navigate life successfully, each of us will need to have vision and focus on the most important aspects of life. When our attention is turned towards the sharks of this world, the waves of fear, the winds of trouble, and all of the other problems that are sure to surround us, we are certainly going to sink. However, if we can maintain a positive focus on the beautiful, healthy, happy things in life, we will become lights to a rather dark and dim world.

It is Easy to Lose Our Focus

Over the years, we have observed many well-meaning, strong, and faithful members of the Church misalign their priorities and lose their focus. We include ourselves in this generalization, as well as members of our own families. We are all guilty of "looking beyond the mark" (Jacob 4:14) and letting the trivial and less important issues take the place of the vital ingredients to a happy life. For example,

- Some people focus on their work and neglect their families.
- Some focus on material possessions and seem less concerned with the people around them.
- Some are more focused on commiserating and complaining rather than finding solutions to their problems.
- Some parents are so focused on ensuring their children turn out perfectly that they are extremely harsh on them. Only later do they learn that their children were actually "pretty darn-good kids."
- Others are so focused on their Church responsibilities that they forget their spouses, children, and grandchildren.
- Some individuals become hyper-focused on the weaknesses of others yet ignore their own addictions and problems.
- Some of our children, and adults, have become so focused on their smartphones that they ignore their families and the precious promptings from the Holy Ghost.
- Some are hyper-focused on what is wrong with the world; unfortunately, they fail to see the good things all around them.

We can unwittingly bring frustration, stress, and sadness into our lives if we are hyper-focused on trivial or less important areas of our lives. For example, we know of a mother who spent excessive amounts of time on keeping her house clean, and she did a wonderful job. Her home was always immaculate. However, along with her passion to have the cleanest home in the neighborhood, she completely neglected her children. Today, as a grandmother of a large posterity, she has marginalized relationships with her family because of the seeds she planted as a young mother. Likewise, we know of a father who spent his entire life focused on his work. Each member of his family, including his wife, recognized that his career was his first priority. As his career progressed and the demands at work became more intense, he completely disconnected from his family. Today, he is an eighty-year-old man. He and his wife divorced over thirty years ago, and he has no relationship with his children or grandchildren. This man certainly worked hard in his life but perhaps directed too much of his energy in the wrong areas.

A Lack of Focus and Our Mental Health

We have tried to underscore throughout this chapter that, a lack of focus, or an inappropriate focus, can be damaging to our mental and emotional health. We know of many individuals whom we see in our private practices that have allowed a "lack of focus" to significantly interfere with their happiness in life. For example, some adults are so focused on the events of the world, newscasts, podcasts, and misinformation from many sources, that they believe the world is coming to an end—tonight—and are living their lives in an utter state of panic. There are others who simply focus on all the negative things in their own personal lives—their failures, disappointments, and shortcomings—only to feel depressed most of the day.

Some individuals try to cope with unmet needs or painful emotions by seeking inappropriate attention and involvement with those of the opposite sex. Consequently, they run the risk of engaging in behavior that is damaging to their marriages and families. Others become focused on pornography, which undermines their ability to build deep, meaningful relationships, including with their own spouses. There are also those who become so focused on technology such as social media and video games that they are unable to engage in real, lasting relationships with their families and friends.

We have also noticed that there are some people who are so much "in their own heads" that they cannot enjoy life, their families, or their work. They are constantly analyzing every conversation and every interaction, completely convinced that they said or did something wrong. These individuals walk on "eggshells" in every relationship, constantly second-guessing their every move. They spend hours trying to apologize for things they said or did that no one is really that concerned about.

Focusing on Jesus Christ

There is a wonderful formula in the scriptures that teaches us where to direct our focus: "Look unto me in every thought; doubt not, fear not" (D&C 6:36). By focusing our lives on Jesus Christ, "all other things fall into their proper place or drop out of our lives."[5] If Christ is our centerpiece, we will see the world in a more optimistic, healthy, and positive way. We believe that if Jesus Christ is our focus, then:

- We can see the good in the world and the beauties that surround us, instead of viewing our environment as a toxic place.
- We can see the talents, gifts, good, and contributions of others, instead of viewing humans as bad people with malicious intentions.
- We can look to the future with hope and faith, instead of with pessimism and negativity.
- We can find joy and fulfillment in our family relationships, instead of focusing on what is wrong with everyone.
- We can live our lives from a paradigm of love, instead of a perspective of fear and worry.

Essentially, if we want to live our lives looking *up* instead of *down*, we should focus on the good that we see all around us. Centering our hearts and minds on the Savior, His teachings, His love, and the blessings He gives us is a great beginning.

Mark shares the following experience that could help illustrate this point:

Several years ago when we lived in the Dallas Metroplex, I was driving from Denton to Lewisville for a work meeting. As I drove, a massive Texas rainstorm hit hard—the kind where you can barely see out of your front windshield. As I was crossing Lake Lewisville on Interstate 35, I heard one of my back tires blow out. After successfully crossing the bridge, I exited off to the right side of the road to assess the damage. The rain was coming down so hard that after only a few minutes of working on my tire, it looked as though I had jumped into a swimming pool with all of my clothes on.

I do not claim to be an expert on changing tires—but I have changed many in my life—perhaps too many. Nevertheless, for some reason, the lug nut wrench in my car did not fit the lug nuts on the tire. I was not sure what I was going to do. I was not wild about hitchhiking, so I decided to start walking down the access road that ran parallel to the Interstate Highway. I knew about a mile up the road was the exit for one of the main roads in Lewisville. I assumed I could at least walk to an auto parts store and purchase the necessary lug nut wrench. I began feeling that life was one big bummer. I was now going to miss my meeting. I felt our finances were so tight that I really could not afford to purchase a new tire. I was beginning to feel a bit sad and depressed. Lately, it felt like too many things always seemed to go wrong. My head was definitely focused on the ground as I began my long walk in a rainstorm, completely drenched.

However, as I began my walk, a man in a red truck pulled up next to me. This strong, cheerful Texan was just what the doctor ordered. He asked if there was anything he could do to help. Feeling a little sheepish, I explained to him that I knew how to change the tire, but the lug nut wrench was the wrong size. He got out of his truck, went back to the bed, and pulled out a cross shaped lug nut wrench. Then, he came over to the car with me, and we placed the wrench on one of the lug nuts—it fit perfectly. He then said to me, "Just keep the wrench." I said, "No, I don't want to take your wrench." My new friend replied, "It's no big deal, I have another one."

I was humbled by this stranger's kindness to me. I thought it was incredibly generous of him to give a complete stranger a $25 lug nut wrench. As he drove away, I was grateful for his compassion. He even offered to help me change the tire, but I let him know that I could do it. He did say he had a meeting in Austin he was trying to get to, and I didn't want to make him late. As I sat in the pouring rain, changing my tire, I wondered *if I would be the type of person who would do something similar for someone else. The darkness began to leave me, and I began to smile as I considered what had just happened to me. I felt that God had sent this stranger to me. I began to look towards the sky with a prayer of thanks.*

As I was completing tire-changing process, the same red truck drove up again. I thought to myself, "He probably had second thoughts about his wrench and came back to get it." Instead, he told me that he had gone back to his house to get me a sweatshirt. It was a freezing cold and rainy day in North Texas, and I was again, dumbfounded that this man would do such a thing.

From the cab of his truck, he tossed me the sweatshirt and I thanked him profusely. I felt bad that he had taken now about thirty minutes out of his work day to take care of a total stranger. This time, as he drove away, my faith and hope in the human race was restored. I expressed another silent prayer heavenward— thank God for people like this man. Even though this experience happened over fifteen years ago, I still have that sweatshirt in my closet to remind me of the kindness of a complete stranger.

When we put our faith in the Savior and notice the "tender mercies" that occur in our lives, it gives us great reason to "look up" and rejoice in the world that we live in. It helps us change our focus from being victims to being children of a loving God who always remembers us. And what about the stranger? Perhaps he was also having a bad day; maybe his marriage or family life wasn't great; perhaps he was traveling to Austin for a work interview. Maybe by helping someone else in need, he was able to put his own problems in perspective. Perhaps he had been somewhat depressed, and now was feeling much better about his life as he traveled south on Interstate 35.

Maintaining a Healthy Life Focus

It is never too late to change. We believe that negative habits, which often take years to acquire, can be reversed with some consistent effort and energy. From a gospel perspective, we should pray to our Father in Heaven to help us have a correct focus. We can ask him to help us "see the right things." We can pray to be more optimistic and more filled with hope.

More specifically, we can pray for the spiritual gifts that will help us to "look up." Part of our existence here on this earth is to acquire and develop our spiritual gifts. We have been encouraged by President George Q. Cannon, who taught,

> How many of you . . . are seeking for these gifts that God has promised to bestow? How many of you, when you bow before your Heavenly Father in your family circle or in your secret places, contend for these gifts to be bestowed upon you? How many of you ask the Father, in the name of Jesus, to manifest Himself to you through these powers and these gifts? Or do you go along day by day, like a door turning on its hinges, without having any feeling upon the subject, without exercising any faith whatever, content to be baptized and be members of the Church and to rest there, thinking that your salvation is secure because you have done this? . . .
>
> If any of us are imperfect, it is our duty to pray for the gift that will make us perfect. Have I imperfections? I am full of them. What is my duty? To pray to God to give me the gifts that will correct these imperfections. If I am an angry man, it is my duty to pray for charity, which suffereth long and is kind. Am I an envious man? It is my duty to seek for charity, which envieth not. So with all the gifts of the gospel. They are intended for this purpose. No man ought to say, "Oh, I cannot help this; it is my nature." He is not justified in it, for the reason that God has promised to give strength to correct these things, and to give gifts that will eradicate them. If a man lack wisdom, it is his duty to ask God for wisdom. The same with everything else. That is the design of God concerning His Church. He wants His Saints to be perfected in the truth.[6]

If we lack faith, then let us pray for the gift of courage; if we are discouraged by the events in the world, let us pray for the gift of hope; if we are constantly negative and critical, we should pray for optimism and happiness. If we are judgmental of others, then we could pray for the gifts of charity and love.

Here are some other suggestions to "look up" and see the good:

1. Look for the good in everything we see or encounter. Sometimes, our own children can be negative in their attitudes towards others. Perhaps they have seen such modeling from their parents who could also be quite negative or critical. Try to find the good in everyone. At President George Albert Smith's funeral, Elder Matthew Cowley, said that President Smith's last message and instruction to him was, "you will find the good in everyone if you will but look for it."[7] George Albert Smith lived true to those words. Many of his contemporaries admired him because he could find the good in every soul. As we look for the good in others, we will begin to fill happiness and peace in our own lives.

2. When seeing so much negativity, take the time to write down the positive. Mark reported that there was a time that some of their children had become so negative that he and Janie decided it was time to do something about it. They gave some of their children a small spiral notebook. Each time they said one negative thing about someone, or complained about something, they were required to write down five positive things to counter the one negative. For adults, this would not be a bad exercise either. Each time you find yourself "looking down" or becoming focused on the negative; write down five positive things about the issue that is challenging you. It will not take long to change your paradigm from negative to positive.

3. Keep your gratitude flowing and growing. You will see us mention gratitude often in this book. Why? Because gratitude is such a powerful antidote for fear, worry, and negativity. Instead of complaining about something, find a reason to be grateful. Mark shared the following experience that taught him a great lesson. After graduating with his master's degree in counseling, he was invited to continue working at the psychiatric hospital where he did his internship. However, he also had his normal full-time job. Therefore, he would work his normal job from 7 a.m. to 3:30 p.m. each day. In addition, he worked at the psychiatric hospital Monday through Wednesday from 4:00 p.m. to 11:00 p.m., which also included being on-call three nights a week, from 11:00 a.m. to 7:00 a.m. Over time, he was becoming tired, exhausted, and worn out. One day, his mother-in-law asked, "Mark, how is your job at the hospital going?" Mark responded that he was tired and exhausted, and that he was tired of working there—almost looking for approval from someone to quit. Then his mother-in-law said, "Isn't it wonderful how Heavenly Father is blessing your family? He has given you this additional income to pay off your graduate school debts. What a blessing this second job has been for you." Mark's attitude changed from one of complaining about a job he did not like to gratitude for the blessing of having a means to pay off debts. For so many of us, life is like that. We often complain about the very things that are blessings sent down from heaven (i.e. our children!). Cultivating an attitude of gratitude is practically a panacea for stress and anxiety.

4. Get outdoors and enjoy some sunshine. When was the last time you marveled at God's creations? Have you ever watched the sun set over a lake? Have you seen the moon behind a mountain peak? Have you been to a waterfall far away from civilization? Have you walked across newly fallen snow? Have you jumped into a cool, refreshing lake on a hot summer day? One study reported that children today spend twice as long looking at screens as playing outside. Specifically, the study reported that by the time they reach the age of seven, children will have looked at screens the equivalent of 456 days—an average of four hours per day. However, these same children will have only spent 182 days, or an hour and a half a day playing outdoors. A *National Trust* research study showed that, on average, children between the ages of 10–16 spend 12.6 minutes a day on vigorous outdoor activities compared to 10.4 waking hours, being relatively motionless. Another study was even more alarming. The average person now spends 93 percent of his life indoors.[8] "That means if you live to be 100, you will have spent 93 of those years in a little compartment and only 7 outside in the dazzling, living world. If we live to the more usual 75, we will spend 69 and three-fourths of our years indoors, and only 5 and one-fourth outside. Author John Eldredge attested:

> This is a catastrophe, the final nail in the coffin for the human soul. You live nearly all your life in a fake world: artificial lighting instead of the warmth of sunlight or the cool of

moonlight or the darkness of night itself. Artificial climate rather than the wild beauty of real weather; your world is always 68 degrees. All of the surfaces you touch are things like plastic, nylon, and faux leather instead of meadow, wood, and stream. Fake fireplaces; wax fruit. The atmosphere you inhibit is now asphyxiating with artificial smells—mostly chemicals and "air fresheners"—instead of cut grass, wood smoke, and salt air (anyone weeping yet?). In place of the cry of the hawk, the thunder of a waterfall, the comfort of crickets, your world spews out artificial sounds—all the clicks and beeps and whir of technology, the hum of the HVAC. Dear God, even the plants in your little bubble are fake. They give no oxygen; instead the plastic off-gases toxins, and if that isn't a signal fire I don't know what is. . . . But this is not the life God ordained for the sons of Adam and the daughters of Eve, whose habitat is this sumptuous earth. It's like putting wild horses in a Styrofoam box for the rest of their lives.[9]

Eldredge went on to explain that living our lives in an artificial world is like being wrapped in plastic. We feel tired, numb, and depressed, and then wonder why. "The simple answer is you have vitamin D deficiency, there's no sunlight in your life, literally and figuratively."[10] Do you want to become reconnected to some positivity in your life? Go on a long bike ride while you listen to your favorite playlist or podcast; ride bikes with your family, hike the natural trails, hills, mountains, and streams in your community; have a barbeque in your backyard; work in your yard as a family.

5. Collect statements of positivity and review them often. That is right, go on a search and rescue mission, and begin to compile all the statements you can on faith, hope, optimism, and happiness. Consider the following examples:

a. President Gordon B. Hinckley said, "Who among us has not felt fear? I know of no one who has been entirely spared. Some are able to rise above it quickly, but others are trapped and pulled down by it and even driven to defeat. [It is critical to] recognize that *fear comes not of God, but rather from the adversary.*"[11]

b. President Thomas S. Monson stated, "My beloved brothers and sisters, fear not. Be of good cheer. The future is as bright as your faith."[12]

c. President Calvin Coolidge said, "If you see ten troubles coming down the road, you can be sure that nine will run into the ditch before they reach you."

What would happen if you collected such statements and then transcribed them on 3 x 5 card, or typed them up on your computer? Then, you could pull them out of your purse or briefcase or backpack or even save them on your phone. If you reviewed these statements several times each day, you would begin to rewire the neural pathways in your brain. Over time, you would be able to overcome your tendency to be negative. A rather large part of your life would be spent "Looking Up" and seeing the beauties of life unfold before your very eyes.[13]

Remember, when Moses sent twelve spies to the Promised Land, ten came back and reported that the land was flowing "with milk and honey" (see Numbers 13:27). However, because of the large amount of inhabitants and "giants" in the land, these spies gave an "evil report" (Numbers 13:32), providing all of the reasons why they *could not* obtain the land. However, two of the spies, Joshua and Caleb, saw things somewhat differently. Yes, they did see the large amount of inhabitants and the same giants, but they also saw the land as "good," and believed the Lord would help them obtain it. Our friend and colleague, Dr. John Hilton III, made this observation:

> All the spies observed the same fruits, lands, fortifications, and people. Some dwelt on the bad, others on the good. Because most Israelites focused on the bad and rebelled against Moses, they wandered in the wilderness for forty years. Joshua and Caleb, the spies who gave the good report, were the only ones who had seen the miracles of Egypt allowed to enter the promised land (see Numbers 14:22–24). We choose what we see. Will we see the delicious fruit or the giant army? The positives or the negatives? Will we be the ten or the two?[14]

Indeed, it is better to look up! Our happiness most often depends on our ability to look up and see the good! Commence to look for the good in others, in your circumstances, and in the world around you. If you can do that, depression, stress, and anxiety will be replaced with happiness, hope, and optimism.

References to Chapter 14

1   Dale Carnegie, *How to Stop Worrying and Start Living* (Simon & Schuster, 1944).

2   Carl B. Cook, "It is Better to Look Up," *Ensign*, November 2011.

3   Randy Alcorn, Florence Chadwick and the Fog, *Eternal Perspective Ministries*; accessed 18 March 22, https://www.epm.org/resources/2010/ Jan/21/florence-chadwick-and-fog. See also https://www.encyclopedia.com/ people/sports-and-games/sports-biographies/florence-may-chadwick.

4   Howard W. Hunter, *Ensign*, November 1992, 19.

5   Ezra Taft Benson, "The Great Commandment—Love the Lord," *Ensign*, May 1988.

6   George Q. Cannon, *Latter-Day Saints Millennial Star*, 23 April 1894, 258–261.

7   Matthew Cowley, *Improvement Era*, June 1951, 405.

8   Neil E. Klepeis at al., "The National Human Activity Pattern Survey (NHAPS): A Resource for Assessing Exposure to Environmental Pollutants," *Journal of Exposure Analysis and Environmental Epidemiology* 11, no. 3 (May-June 2001): 231–252.

9   John Eldredge, *Get Your Life Back: Everyday Practices in a World Gone Mad* [Nashville, Tennessee: Nelson Books, 2020], 77.

10   Eldredge, 78.

11   Gordon B. Hinckley, "God Hath Not Given Us the Spirit of Fear," *Ensign*, October 1984, 2.

12   Thomas S. Monson, "Be of Good Cheer," *Ensign*, May 2009, 92.

13   Jeffrey R. Holland, "Cast Not Away Therefore Your Confidence," Ensign, June 2000.

14   Dr. John Hilton III, *The Founder of Our Peace*, (Salt Lake City: Deseret Book, 2020), 36.

Chapter 15

RELYING ON THE PRINCE OF PEACE

And the peace of God, which passeth all
understanding, shall keep your hearts
and minds through Christ Jesus.[1]

LIVING IN THE present, making peace with the past, developing optimism and self-compassion, overcoming perfectionism, managing stress, and so on—they all have their place on the table of peace. More important than any of these, however, is the gift of peace that we can receive from the author of peace, even Jesus Christ, the "Prince of Peace." His is the peace that comes from Heavenly power, from the Atonement of Jesus Christ, and is only His to give: "Peace I leave with you, my peace I give unto you: not as the world giveth, give I unto you. Let not your heart be troubled, neither let it be afraid" (John 14:27).

How do we obtain this peace, the peace of Christ, that will overshadow the troubles and fears we experience in the world? The answer to this question lies in our willingness to believe His words and to draw closer to Him.

Come Unto Me

In the New Testament the Savior extended an invitation to all of us. He stated, "Come unto me, all ye that labour and are heavy laden, and I will give you rest. Take my yoke upon you, and learn of me; for I am meek and lowly in heart: and ye shall find rest unto your souls. For my yoke is easy, and my burden is light" (Matthew 11:28–30).

In these verses, the Lord promises rest to our souls and to lighten our burdens if we will yoke ourselves to him. In other words, He will share our challenges, pains, sins, and the weight of our respective trials if we come unto Him. How does that happen? President Howard W. Hunter explained,

> In biblical times the yoke was a device of great assistance to those who tilled the field. It allowed the strength of a second animal to be linked and coupled with the effort of a single animal, sharing and reducing the heavy labor of the plow or wagon. A burden that was overwhelming or perhaps impossible for one to bear could be equitably and comfortably borne by two bound together with a common yoke. . . .
>
> Why face life's burdens alone, Christ asks, or why face them with temporal support that will quickly falter? To the heavy laden it is Christ's yoke, it is the power and peace of standing side by side with a God that will provide the support, balance, and strength to meet our challenges and endure our tasks here in the hardpan field of mortality.[2]

Elder Gerald Lund added this insight:

One last note of interest about yokes, especially those made for oxen. Yokes are not mass produced. Each yoke is made for a specific pair of animals. The yoke has to fit the neck and shoulders just right or it will chafe the animals and reduce their ability to pull. Oxen are not the same size, weight, and height. If the yoke is not made to accommodate that difference, then the larger ox may drag the smaller one to some extent, or throw him off balance. I love that concept.

When I come to the Savior with my burdens, my problems, and my challenges, He doesn't hand me an off-the-shelf-one-size-fits-all-yoke. He knows me intimately. He loves me infinitely. Therefore, the help that he offers me will be perfectly fitted to my needs, my abilities, and my circumstances. How profound are those words: "Take my yoke upon you."[3]

The first step to yoking ourselves with the Savior is to believe that He is there, that He lives, that He loves us, and that He wants to help us. In this matter, our belief may be strong, or it might be waning or not exist at all.

To develop a belief in God and a relationship with Him, we need to learn about Him. First, we can go directly to the well of living water—the scriptures—to learn of Jesus Christ. Next, we can study what prophets, both present and past, have said about Him. Success in this process will require actively seeking to understand who He is, His teachings and doctrine, His covenants, and the promises He has made to those who wish to follow Him. The Apostle Paul taught, "Faith cometh by hearing, and hearing by the word of God" (Romans 10:17), and "for he that cometh to God must believe that he is, and *that* he is a rewarder of them that diligently seek him" (Hebrews 11:6). In modern times, the Lord has said, "Draw near unto me and I will draw near unto you; seek me diligently and ye shall find me; ask, and ye shall receive; knock, and it shall be opened unto you." (D&C 88:63). To increase our faith, it is necessary for us to diligently seek Him by studying, pondering, and acting on His words.

Coming to know Our Father in Heaven and His Son, Jesus Christ, also requires enough belief or at least enough desire to believe to offer heartfelt prayers to Him. Such prayers include open expressions of honest feelings, needs, and desires and to have experiences with Him. President Russell M. Nelson has described this process:

If you are not sure you even believe in God, start there. Understand that in the absence of experiences with God, one can doubt the existence of God. So, put yourself in a position to begin having experiences with Him. Humble yourself. Pray to have eyes to see God's hand in your life and in the world around you. Ask Him to tell you if He is really there—if

He knows you. Ask Him how He feels about you. And then listen.[4]

Our efforts to develop or strengthen our faith in God can be helped greatly as we consider who He is and our familial relationship to him. The doctrine of the restored gospel teaches that God is literally the Father of our Spirits and that we lived with Him before this life. Each of us is, in fact, a beloved Daughter or Son of God for whom He has infinite love. Knowing this and understanding that His greatest desire is to bless us can give us the faith and courage to turn to Him for help and guidance. In fact, it pains Him when we do not trust Him enough to turn to him when we are in need. While addressing an audience at Brigham Young University, Elder Jeffrey R. Holland observed,

> I can tell you this as a parent: As concerned as I would be if somewhere in their lives one of my children were seriously troubled or unhappy or disobedient, nevertheless I would be infinitely more devastated if I felt that at such a time that child could not trust me to help, or should feel his or her interest were unimportant to me or unsafe in my care. In that same spirit, I am convinced that none of us can appreciate how deeply it wounds the loving heart of the Savior of the world when he finds that his people do not feel confident in his care or secure in his hands or trust in his commandments.
>
> Just because God is God, just because Christ is Christ, they cannot do other than care for us and bless us and help us if we will but come unto them, approaching their throne of grace in meekness and lowliness of heart. They can't help but bless us. They have to. It is their nature.[5]

Our hesitancy to "come unto him" may lie in our view of ourselves as not being good enough or worthy of His assistance because of our weaknesses, flaws and sins. At times we may be discouraged or disillusioned because we are painfully aware that we are lacking in so many ways. No matter where we find ourselves, what our experiences have been, or what we think of ourselves, the Lord stands ready to offer acceptance and hope. Elder Dieter F. Uchtdorf offered this insight:

> Sometimes we feel discouraged because we are not "more" of something—more spiritual, respected, intelligent, healthy, rich, friendly, or capable. . . . I learned in my life that we don't need to be "more" of anything to start to become the person God intended us to become. God will take you as you are at this very moment and begin to work with you. All you need is a willing heart, a desire to believe, and trust in the Lord.[6]

Indeed, our Heavenly Father and Jesus Christ accept us as we are. They love us unconditionally and they are anxious to heal us, help us, and bless us.

Trust in the Lord

A few years ago Ted and his wife, Laura, had the following experience:

> *We took a trip with our daughter to visit some of the areas where she had served on her mission the previous year. In one of the communities we visited, there was a member, a former bishop, who invited us to take a ride in his four-seat airplane. This sounded kind of exciting, so we jumped in the plane and took off. Partway through the flight we ran into some turbulence, which made all of us a little nervous. Sensing our anxiety he turned to us and said, "Trust me, I have been through this before and we will be okay." Although we felt reassured, we were still a little uncomfortable. A few minutes later he told us he was turning control of the airplane over to our daughter who was sitting in the front seat next to him. I must admit, I was more anxious at this point than when we had encountered the turbulence. Once again, sensing our upsurge in anxiety, he calmly said, "Trust me, I think she can fly the plane, and I am right here ready to take over if anything happens." Although still nervous, both my wife and I believed he was an honest and wise man who was capable*

of taking over the plane, so we were able to grit our teeth until he once again took control of the plane.

This story underscores the necessity of trusting others as we make our way through life. Trust sometimes can be difficult. Most of us have had many experiences with trust, beginning in childhood, when we trusted and relied on our parents, teachers, and other adults. Each day we put our trust in government leaders, healthcare professionals, mechanics, pilots, and other drivers, to name a few, believing that they will fulfill their promises and obligations.

The most important person for us to learn to trust is the person who knows us best and who is in the position to help us the most, and that is our Heavenly Father. However, developing trust in God takes time and is not always easy. Consider that one-third of the hosts of heaven did not trust God the Father enough to accept His plan in the pre-earth life. Some people, probably because of painful experiences with parents or authority figures, only trust and rely on themselves and no one else. As we work to trust God there may be questions that come to mind such as the following:

- Is He really there?
- Does He know me?
- Does He really care about me?
- Does He really understand and empathize with me?
- Does He want to help or does He think I should do it by myself?
- Am I really worthy of His help? Worth His time and attention?
- If I trust and rely on Him, will He expect too much?
- Will I still have my agency? Will He try to control me?

If we trust that God understands our needs and struggles, wants to help us, has our best interests in mind, and can help us, then we can confidently rely on him to keep His promises and to give us grace, strength, hope and peace. This knowledge enabled Alma to confidently tell his son, Helaman, "for I do know that whosoever shall put their trust in God shall be supported in their trials, and their afflictions, and shall be lifted up at the last day" (Alma 36:3).

Like developing faith, learning to trust God involves hearing and studying the words of those who know and trust him. For example, President Ezra Taft Benson declared, "Nothing is going to startle us more when we pass through the veil to the other side than to realize how well we know our Father and how familiar his face is to us."[7]

Part of our mortal sojourn here on earth is to learn to trust in our Heavenly Father, to let Him lead the way. We must trust Him enough to follow Him, and to believe on His words—especially the promises He has made to us.

Let God Prevail

The more connected we feel to God, the more we will be able to trust him. As our trust grows, so also does our love for him and our desire to be obedient and to align our will with His. Aligning our will with God's is a gradual process of educating our desires, intentions and thoughts to be more like His and being willing to yield our hearts to God. King Benjamin described it as putting off the natural man and becoming "a saint through the Atonement of Christ the Lord, and [becoming] as a child, submissive, meek, humble, patient, full of love, and willing to submit to all things which the Lord seeth fit to inflict upon [us], even a child doeth submit to his father (Mosiah 3:19).

In the October 2021 General Conference of the Church, President Russell M. Nelson spoke on letting God prevail in our lives. In that address, he asked a series of questions to help us understand what that means and where each of us is in that process:

- Are you willing to let God prevail in your life?
- Are you willing to let God be the most important influence in your life?
- Will you allow His words, His commandments, and His covenants to influence what you do each day?
- Will you allow His voice to take priority over any other?
- Are you willing to let whatever He needs you to do take precedence over every other ambition?
- Are you willing to have your will swallowed up in His?[8]

These are searching questions that focus on our willingness to put God first and let His will prevail in our lives. Submitting our will to His is not easy and requires faith that He knows what is best for us, that the things he asks us to do are for our good, and that our happiness and success is His greatest desire. In essence, having the faith that aligning our will with His will allows us to progress and become as He is. Elder Neal A. Maxwell described what he felt was the essence of submitting our will to the will of the Lord:

> The submission of one's will is really the only uniquely personal thing we have to place on God's altar. It is a hard doctrine, but it is true. The many other things we give to God, however nice that may be of us, are actually things He has already given us, and He has loaned them to us. But when we begin to submit ourselves by letting our wills be swallowed up in God's will, then we are really giving something to Him. And that hard doctrine lies at the center of discipleship. There is a part of us that is ultimately sovereign, the mind and heart, where we really do decide which way to go and what to do. And when we submit to His will, then we've really given Him the one thing He asks of us. And the other things are not very, very important. It is the only possession we have that we can give, and there is no resulting shortage in our agency as a result. Instead, what we see is a flowering of our talents and more and more surges of joy. Submission to Him is the only form of submission that is completely safe.[9]

Submitting our will to God's does not come naturally to most of us and can seem quite daunting when we consider what might be involved in being willing to do whatever the Lord might ask of us. Fortunately, the Lord is patient and is willing to give us opportunities to learn how to align our desires with His.

For example, Elder Robert C. Gay of the Seventy shared an experience that he and his wife, Lynette, had with a member of the Quorum of the Twelve that helped them learn a valuable lesson about living their lives according to God's priorities. Elder Gay was interviewed by a Senior member of the Quorum of the Twelve Apostles and asked to serve as a mission president. His experience was recounted in the *Church News*:

> At the time, Elder and Sister Gay had challenging family dynamics and were heavily involved in large humanitarian efforts. He was also a senior managing partner of a global investment business. They determined it wouldn't be the best time for them to serve. Without hesitation, the apostle said to Elder Gay, "You really don't get it. The Lord is calling you to save your life. You are either going to live your life by covenant or convenience. There is never a convenient time to serve."
>
> Elder Gay was stunned. He and Sister Gay went home and prayerfully considered how they would live their lives. "We quickly made the choice to serve and live our lives by covenant, doing whatsoever things the Lord asked of us," Elder Gay said. "Our lives have not been the same since."[10]

If our desire is to let God prevail in our lives, and if we ask for it, the Lord will give us experiences, gifts, and grace to help us to accomplish that goal.

Personalizing the Atonement of Jesus Christ

Not long ago a man we know had a conversation with a friend who had decided to leave the church. In the course of their discussion, the man said, "The church has clearly been working for you, but it has not been working for me." Implicit in his statement was his further belief that the Atonement of Jesus Christ had not been working in his life either. He had not been experiencing the power of the Savior's Atonement to cleanse him from sin, to give him strength to face adversity and affliction, to heal him spiritually and emotionally, and to obtain Christlike personal qualities.

Unfortunately, there are members of the church who believe in Jesus Christ but who do not think that the redeeming, strengthening, and transforming power of His Atonement can operate in their lives. Perhaps they feel that their problems are not important enough for the Lord to care about or that they are unworthy or underserving of His help or that they lack the necessary faith to receive His promised blessings.

When the Savior walked the earth, much of His time was spent ministering to people individually—one by one. Those he taught, healed, and forgave came from all walks of life, but many were from the humble classes of society and were often overlooked or deemed unworthy by their peers. The common thread among most of those he helped was that they reached out to Him even if they could exercise only a small degree of faith.

This was the case of a father who asked the Savior to heal his child. The Savior's response was, "If thou canst believe, all things are possible to him that believeth. And straightway the father of the child cried out, and said with tears, Lord, I believe; help thou mine unbelief" (Mark 9:23–24). Though weak in faith, this man had believed enough to ask, and the Lord was merciful and healed his child. Commenting on this account, Elder David A. Bednar offered this thought:

> I wonder if the intent of the man's pleading was not primarily to help him believe in Jesus as our Redeemer and in His healing power. He already may have acknowledged Christ as the Son of God. But perhaps he needed help to believe the Master's healing power indeed could be so individual and so personalized as to bless his own beloved son. He may have believed in Christ generally but not believed Christ specifically and personally.[11]

No matter our station in life, our level of worthiness, what circumstances we are in, or how weak our faith may be, the Lord always responds to those who seek his help. He knows us by name and understands who we are and the challenges, desires, and needs that we encounter. He also ministers to us one person at a time, and the power of His Atonement can be mobilized for all who sincerely desire and ask for it.

In connection with this, President Dallin A. Oaks taught, "Because of His atoning experience in mortality, our Savior is able to comfort, heal, and strengthen all men and women everywhere, but I believe He does so only for those who seek Him and ask for His help."[12] Interestingly, in the course of that address in General Conference, President Oaks mentioned four additional times that the blessings of the Atonement of Jesus Christ come to those who *ask* for help.

If we do seek Him and ask for his help, the Savior offers His love and the blessings of His Atonement to help us change, to become better versions of ourselves, to have the strength to deal with adversity, and the ability to accomplish more than we could ever achieve on our own. This assurance brings us hope, confidence, and peace.

While the Lord will respond to our requests for help, and always has our best interests in mind, he will do it in the way that He feels is best and on His own timetable. Ted learned this important lesson through his own experience of dealing with anxiety. He explains,

Throughout my growing up years, I had a problem with anxiety, which reached its apex when I was a teenager. What was termed "stage fright," now known as social anxiety, was a painful part of my existence. I was okay while interacting with others one-on-one or in small groups of people whom I knew well, but if asked to speak in front of a group, my anxiety was astronomical and completely debilitating. I was petrified if I had to give an oral report or in any way speak in front of the class in high school. The same was true if I was asked to give a short talk in sacrament meeting. I would avoid doing those things at all costs, but the few times where I had to do it, my anxiety was so high that my voice would crack, I would shake physically, and it was evident to members of the congregation that I was terrified. This, of course, was the source of a great deal of embarrassment and shame to me.

I am very nearsighted and have worn glasses or contact lenses since I was six years old. I even had the idea of taking my glasses off when I had to speak in front of others so I wouldn't be able to see them and, hopefully, not feel as scared. As you might guess, that did not work too well because, even though I could not see them well, I still knew that people were there and they were looking at me.

When it came time to serve a mission, I was not sure I could do it because I understood that as a missionary I would have to teach people I did not know, I would have to speak in church, and I would probably have to speak in front of others in missionary meetings. This was daunting to me, but I decided it was best to go forward with the hope that I could get through it without too much anguish. I enjoyed serving as a missionary, but as expected, I also had times where my anxiety reared its head and interfered with both my performance and my sense of well-being. At some point in my missionary service, I came to understand and believe that the Lord would actually help me to overcome my weaknesses and insecurities if I had enough faith to ask him. I had heard this repeated over the pulpit and in church classes for many years and believed it generally but did not really think it applied to me in a personal way.

So, I started to ask my Heavenly Father to help me with my problem with anxiety. It was a slow process, but over the years things have improved significantly. I believe the Lord has given me opportunities and experiences, including some time in therapy, that, along with His grace and the healing power of the Savior's Atonement, have helped me to overcome this problem. I still get anxious sometimes when speaking in front of others, but it does not interfere with my ability to communicate and, in fact, helps me to do a better job in most cases.

The peace that the Savior promises us, His peace, can be present for each of us as we respond to His invitation to "come unto Him," and as we learn to trust and exercise faith in Him. Moreover, allowing God to prevail in our lives, seeking to put His will above ours, and asking for the power of His Atonement to operate on our behalf will most assuredly enable us to experience his love, his sustaining influence, his healing, his redemption, his comfort, his acceptance, his grace, and ultimately his peace "which passeth all understanding."[13]

References to Chapter 15

1 Philippians 4:7

2 Howard W. Hunter, *Ensign*, November 1990, 18.

3 Gerald N. Lund, *Divine Signatures*, (Salt Lake City: Deseret Book, 2010), 202–204.

4 Russell M. Nelson, "Come Follow Me," *Ensign,* May 2019.

5 Jeffrey R. Holland, "Come Unto Him," BYU Speeches, March 2, 1997.

6 Dieter F. Uchtdorf, "It Works Wonderfully," *Ensign*, May 2015.

7 Ezra Taft Benson, "Jesus Christ—Gifts and Expectations," BYU Speeches, 1975, p. 313.

8 Russell M. Nelson, "Let God Prevail," *Ensign,* November 2015.

9 Neal A. Maxwell, "Sharing Insights from My Life," BYU Devotional, January 12, 1999.

10 Sydney Walker, "How are you driving your life? Elder and Sister Gay ask young adults during worldwide devotional," *Church News*, May 3, 2020.

11 David A. Bednar, "If Ye Had Known Me," *Ensign*, November 2016.

12 Dallin H. Oaks, "Strengthened by the Atonement of Jesus Christ," *Ensign*, November 2015.

13 Philippians 4:7

TED P. ASAY

TED P. ASAY is a Clinical Psychologist in private practice in Dallas, Texas. He works with adults, adolescents and children who struggle with depression, anxiety, stress and trauma.

Ted is also Clinical Assistant Professor of Psychiatry at the University of Texas Southwestern Medical Center where he teaches graduate classes and supervises students. He received both a Bachelor of Science degree in psychology and a doctor of philosophy degree in clinical psychology from Brigham Young University.

MARK D. OGLETREE

MARK D. OGLETREE joined the Church at age eighteen. He served an LDS mission from 1982 to 1984 in Seattle, Washington. He earned a bachelor of arts degree in 1987 from Brigham Young University, a master of arts in educational psychology from Northern Arizona University in 1990, a master of arts in mental health counseling in 1994 from Northern Arizona University, and a PhD in family and human development from Utah State University in May 2000.

Mark has taught at Brigham Young University in the Church History and Doctrine Department since 2010. He has published several books and articles on marriage and family relationships.

~ NOTES ~

~ NOTES ~

~ NOTES ~

~ NOTES ~

~ NOTES ~

~ NOTES ~

~ NOTES ~

~ NOTES ~

~ NOTES ~

~ NOTES ~

~ NOTES ~

AUTHORS WANTED

You've dreamed of accomplishing your publishing goal for ages—holding *that* book in your hands. We want to partner with you in bringing this dream to light.

Whether you're an aspiring author looking to publish your first book or a seasoned author who's been published before, we want to hear from you. Please submit your manuscript to:

CEDARFORT.SUBMITTABLE.COM/SUBMIT

CEDAR FORT
Publishing & Media

**CEDAR FORT IS CURRENTLY PUBLISHING
BOOKS IN THE FOLLOWING GENRES:**

- LDS Nonfiction
- General Nonfiction
- Cookbooks
- Children's
- Biographies
- Self-Help
- Comic & Activity books
- Children's books with customizable characters